66 PASSAGES

TO LEARN TO READ BETTER

Second Edition

A Course for Understanding
The Basic Structure Of
The Sentence
The Paragraph
The Short Passage

By

Allan Sack

Formerly: Director, College Skills Center and Speed Reading Institute; Supervisor, Adult Reading Laboratory, College of the City of New York; Lecturer, Reading, Study Skills and Vocabulary Development, Extension Division and Graduate School of Business Administration, Rutgers University; American Institute of Banking; Currently: Consultant on Teacher Training.

Jack Yourman

Clinical Psychologist; Formerly Director, College Skills Center and Speed Reading Institute. Consultant, New York Telephone Co., Port of New York Authority, United Nations Lecturer, Rutgers University, American Institute of Banking; Associate Professor, Fordham University. Currently: Consultant, I.B.M., International Paper Company.

AGS®

American Guidance Service, Circle Pines, Minnesota 55014-1796

Other College Skills Books That Help to Increase Reading Ability:

88 Passages to Develop Reading Comprehension

Highly interesting and informative reading selections for teenagers and adults. Includes instruction in identifying the logical structure of a passage. Comprehension is developed through multiple-choice questions that exercise six fundamental skills.

100 Passages to Develop Reading Comprehension

100 challenging short passages from a wide range of interest areas. Uses an analytical method that enables better readers to become accomplished readers.

The Sack-Yourman Developmental Speed Reading Course

Develops speed, comprehension, retention, and concentration by analyzing the thought content and structure of articles. No gimmicks or gadgets.

Editor: Barbara Pokrinchak, Ed.D.
Editorial Consultant: H. F. Criste

Printed in the United States of America.
A 0 9 8 7 6 5 4 3 2

ISBN: 0-89026-660-3

Order Number: 82750

CONTENTS

Part One is the **theory**—the basic ideas you need to understand reading.

Part Two is the **practice**—passages to read and questions to answer to develop your ability to use the theory.

Note: For answers to the questions, analyses of the passages, and grade levels, see the *Teacher's Manual for 66 Passages.*

PART ONE: WHAT THE STUDENT NEEDS TO KNOW TO READ BETTER

Instruction Page

These left-hand pages give instructions for what the student is to do. The student carries out these instructions on the right-hand pages. These instructions for teaching Part One have been taken directly from the *Teacher's Manual.* This provides the more advanced student an opportunity to work through Part One independently of the teacher. However, the teacher should be certain before the section is assigned on a self-administered basis that the student's decoding and vocabulary skills are adequate for the job. Instructions for subsequent lessons will be found in the *Manual.*

---

1. TEACHER:

"Someone once said that "when you read, you think."

Once you know what the *words* mean, reading is mainly putting them together — putting them into thoughts.

If reading *is* mainly thinking, and you want to read better, it will pay you to understand how the thinking in reading works. So let's look at how a person thinks when he reads.

▶ Look at the sentence in Part 1 on page 5: "The horse has helped man do his work."

Now, before this sentence could be written for you to read, the author had to start with a TOPIC — he had to have something to write *about.*

▶ Find the topic in this sentence. Draw one line under the topic.

Answer: The topic is "the horse."

Once the writer knows what he wants to write about, the next thing he needs to know is: "What am I going to say about it?" In this sentence he needs to make a STATEMENT about "the horse."

▶ Draw two lines under the statement about the topic, horse.

---

2. ▶ Look at Part 2. The sentence breaks down into two parts: the topic, plus the statement about the topic.

"The horse" "has helped man do his work."

---

3. The TOPIC, as you know, is also called the SUBJECT of the sentence. Look at Part 3. You see three sentences.

▶ Read each sentence. Then draw one line under the subject of each sentence. Answers: The dog. A house. A car.

PART ONE: WHAT YOU NEED TO KNOW ABOUT READING

Student's Page

1.

The horse has helped man do his work.

Directions: Read the sentence above.
Draw one line under the topic.
Draw two lines under the statement about the topic.

2.

TOPIC	+	STATEMENT ABOUT THE TOPIC
The horse		has helped man do his work.

3.

Directions: Read each sentence below.
Draw one line under the subject of each sentence.

The dog is a smart animal.

A house needs to be kept up.

A car needs tune-ups.

4.

Sentences, of course, are the basic building blocks for writing something that will be read. A sentence always is *about* something — its SUBJECT — and always has a STATEMENT about the SUBJECT. The form of a sentence may vary. But the SUBJECT — and the STATEMENT about it — are always there.

Now you also know that what you read doesn't just have single sentences, coming at you one by one on a page. The sentences come at you in groups which you know as paragraphs.

THE PARAGRAPH

So, how do get from the sentence to the paragraph?

▶ Look at Part 4. Read the sentences. Then answer the questions.

Do they all tell about the same subject?	No.
Do they all tell about different subjects?	Yes
Are these sentences a paragraph?	Of course not.

The item in Part 4 is just a bunch of hit-or-miss sentences that have nothing to do with each other. A paragraph must have sentences that *are connected with each other in some logical way.*

5.

Let's go back to the original sentence again. Look at Part 5.

We have here a perfectly good sentence. But as it stands, we may believe what it says, or not. We don't see any *proof* that what it says is true.

It also isn't really clear. What kind of work? *All* man's work? Some of it? We don't know. And the sentence isn't all that interesting. "The horse has helped man do his work." So what else is new? This sentence, then, as a communication between two human beings, is pretty incomplete.

What's needed is some "for instances," some specifics — some EXAMPLES of the work the horse helped man do.

So, let's make a paragraph based on our sentence that might improve its communication value.

6.

▶ Look at Part 6. Read the paragraph. What do sentences 2, 3, and 4 tell about?

Answer: Sentences 2, 3, and 4 tell what *specific kinds* of work the horses did. In other words, sentence 1 makes a general statement about the horse. Sentences 2, 3, and 4 give DETAILS about that general statement.

4.

The horse has helped man do his work. Cars go faster than horses. Bridges help man to cross rivers. My father bought a dog yesterday. In these days the moon isn't that far off.

Directions: Read the sentences above.

Do they all tell about the same subject?	Yes	No
Do they all tell about different subjects?	Yes	No
Are these sentences a paragraph?	Yes	No

5.

The horse has helped man do his work.

6.

(1) The horse has helped man do his work. (2) On Western ranches the horse has helped round up the cattle. (3) Horses moved railroad cars in the early days of the railroad. (4) Horses have pulled brewery trucks.

Directions: Read the paragraph above.
What do sentences 2, 3, and 4 tell about?

____

7.

▶ Look at Part 7, "How Our Paragraph is Built."

Now, let's think about the structure of our paragraph, how it is built, how it is put together.

Our paragraph has a general statement. It has three detail sentences. Each sentence in the paragraph has something to do with what it is about — its SUBJECT.

We call the subject of the paragraph its "SUBJECT MATTER," or "SM."

We call the general statement the "G."

We call the sentences that give details, D's."

Notice that by adding the three DETAILS, we gave the message more "body." The original sentence is now more believable. It is quite clear as to the kinds of work meant. And it might even be a bit more interesting than the sentence we started out with.

8.

Actually, even a *sentence* can have DETAILS. In fact, most sentences do.

For example, let's take the sentence in Part 8.

"They found peace in Shangri-la."

▶ Read the directions and underline your answers.

The SUBJECT is "They."
The STATEMENT about the SUBJECT is "They found peace."
Now, where did "they find peace?" "In Shangri-la." The phrase "in Shangri-la" is a DETAIL which gives more "body" to the sentence, and makes it clearer and more believable.

9.

▶ Look at the sentence in Part 9:

"They fell in love in the springtime."

SUBJECT: "They"
STATEMENT: "They fell in love"
DETAIL (answers "when?"); "in the springtime"

So the SM-G-D format applies to sentences as well as to paragraphs.

7.

HOW OUR PARAGRAPH IS BUILT

SUBJECT MATTER	(SM)	"The horse"
GENERAL STATEMENT	(G)	The horse has helped man do his work.
DETAIL SENTENCES	(D)	On Western ranches the horse has helped round up the cattle.
	(D)	Horses moved railroad cars in the early days of the railroads.
	(D)	Horses have pulled brewery trucks.

8.

They found peace in Shangri-la.

Directions: Read this sentence. What is the subject?
Draw *one* line under the subject.
What is the statement?
Draw *two* lines under the statement.
Where did they find peace?
Draw *three* lines under the words that tell where.

9.

They fell in love in the springtime.

SUBJECT: They

STATEMENT: They fell in love.

DETAIL: in the springtime.

10.

A.

Let's look at our paragraph once again. You can see it in Part 10A. It has a SUBJECT MATTER, a GENERAL STATEMENT, and DETAILS; in other words, it has *parts*. We are saying that a paragraph is built up of parts.

Anything that is built up of parts is a STRUCTURE.

A paragraph is a structure that's built up of thoughts — the kinds of thoughts that we are talking about here.

Each of the "thought-parts" in a paragraph is related to the other parts of the paragraph:

> The GENERAL STATEMENT and the DETAILS are about the SUBJECT MATTER.
>
> The DETAILS support (prove, clarify, or make interesting) the GENERAL STATEMENT.
>
> And the G — the general statement — is related to its supporting DETAILS in a certain way.

B. VISUALIZING THE PARAGRAPH STRUCTURE

If you look at Part 10B, you will see one way of visualizing the structure of a paragraph.

Notice that the SUBJECT MATTER is what is being talked about, in this case, "the horse."

So everything inside the outer border is about "the horse."

The horizontal block is the GENERAL STATEMENT, (G). It is a statement about the SUBJECT MATTER and is written inside the area of the subject matter.

The D's, or DETAILS, support the GENERAL STATEMENT block. Take away the D-supports, and the G-block falls.

10.

A. A Paragraph

The horse has helped man do his work. On Western ranches the horse has helped round up the cattle. Horses moved railroad cars in the early days of the railroads. Horses have pulled brewery trucks.

B. A paragraph has structure.

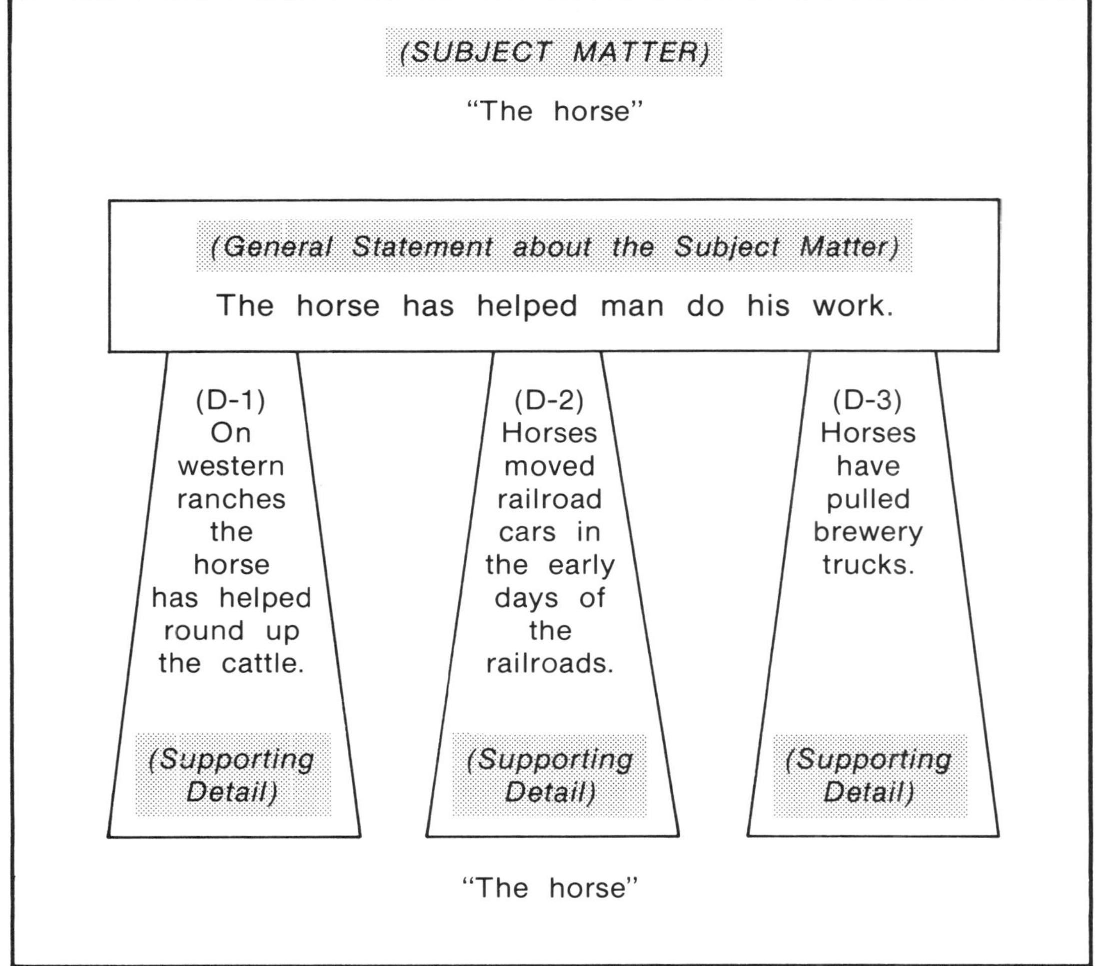

PRACTICAL APPLICATION OF PARAGRAPH STRUCTURE

11.

Now let's see how you can use this SM-G-D idea about how a paragraph is constructed. Let's start with DETAILS.

▶ Look at the paragraph in Part 11.

When you read this, you will see that it is about the taboo in the life of Eskimos... A taboo, if you don't know this word, is a "no-no." If a taboo is placed on some act, that act cannot be done. It is forbidden. Sometimes it cannot even be mentioned or discussed.

▶ Read the paragraph and then we'll talk about it.

. . . .

The SUBJECT MATTER of the paragraph is:

"The taboo in the Eskimo's life."

The G-STATEMENT of the paragraph is:

"The taboo was important in the Eskimo's life."

▶ Read the directions.

The paragraph has three DETAILS. It tells about three kinds of taboos. On the blank line for each DETAIL below, write the numbers of the sentences that make up that DETAIL.

Answers: D-1: Sentences 4 and 5.
D-2: Sentences 6 and 7.
D-3: Sentence 8

12.

Now let's try to spot another set of DETAILS.

▶ Read the directions for Part 12:

Read this paragraph. Find two DETAILS. On the blank line for each DETAIL below, write the numbers of the sentences that make up that DETAIL.

Answers: D-1: Sentences 2, 3, and 4.
D-2: Sentences 5 and 6.

11.

(1) Taboos were an important part of the Eskimo's life. (2) They were rules that came from the spirits around him. (3) He feared the spirits, so he obeyed the taboos. (4) If his wife were sick, it was taboo to spear the salmon. (5) If he did, the salmon would not let itself be caught. (6) If a person died, it was taboo to touch the body with bare hands. (7) If he did, he would sicken and die. (8) He would never, no matter how many days he had gone without food, eat the animal of his totem; it was taboo.

Directions: The paragraph has three DETAILS. It tells about three kinds of taboos. On the blank line for each DETAIL below, write the numbers of the sentences that make up that DETAIL.

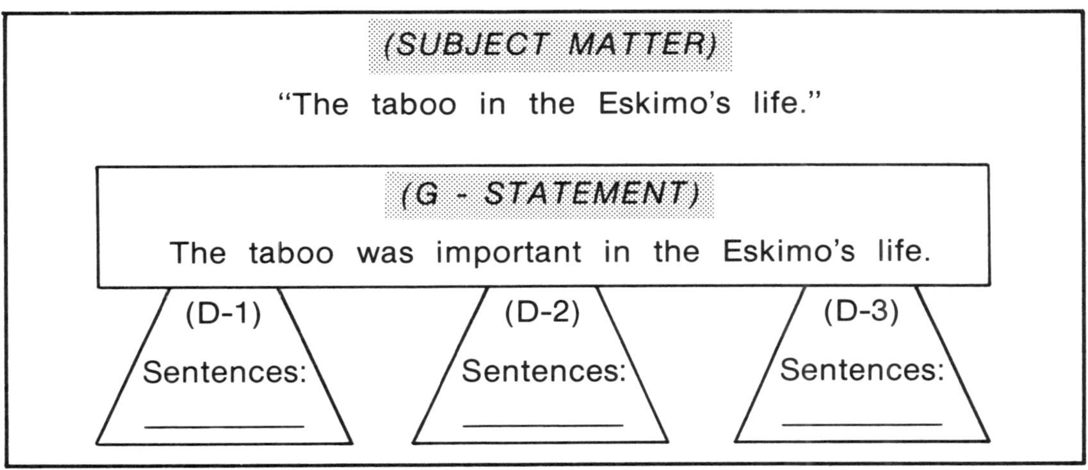

12.

Directions: Read this paragraph. Find two DETAILS. On the blank line for each DETAIL below, write the numbers of the sentences that make up that DETAIL.

(1) "Bulls by nature are dangerous to a cowboy. (2) A bull like Mighty Mouse, or Double Ought, weighs about 1,700 pounds. (3) I weigh 150 pounds. (4) I could get crushed. (5) Their horns go through guys. (6) I've seen it happen."

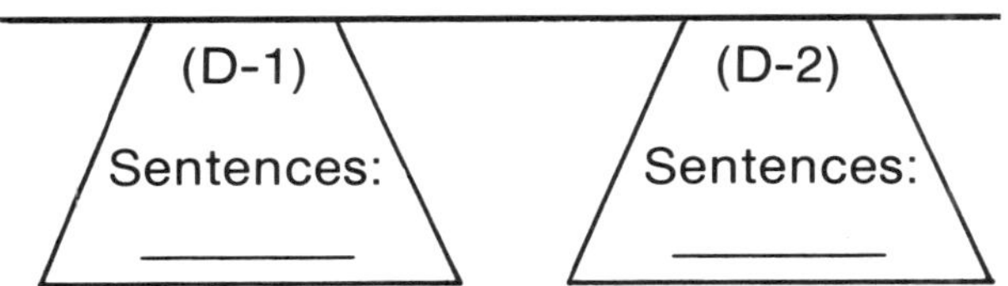

---

13. Now let's talk about THE SUBJECT MATTER.

We said that the SUBJECT MATTER of a paragraph is "What the paragraph is about."

It will pay you to break down this idea of "what it is about" a bit further so that you can open up a number of passages that might otherwise give you trouble. If you understand the SUBJECT MATTER idea clearly, it will also help you later on to study better.

In other words, if you can see the *exact* SUBJECT MATTER of a paragraph, it can be the most important step you can take in understanding the paragraph.

▶ Look at Part 13. Our "Eskimo" passage is, of course, about "Eskimos." That is, it's not about Indians, white trappers, wolves, or seals. You can think of the SUBJECT MATTER of a paragraph as creating a world of its own.

Our SUBJECT MATTER, or SM, is the hunk of the world that we are concerned about when we read the paragraph. We are not talking about anything outside that world. If we do pull in something from outside, it's pulled in only as it affects, or concerns, or is in some way connected with, our SM world.

---

14. But when we say "Our SM is Eskimos," we are talking about a pretty large world. Stories and facts about Eskimos could fill a lot of books. In a paragraph — or a short passage — we can really only talk about one little part of the Eskimo world.

There are all kinds of divisions within the world of "Eskimos." We could talk about the different Eskimo tribes, about their language, about their foods, their religion, and so on.

▶ In Part 14 you can see these parts, or divisions of the *general* SUBJECT MATTER "Eskimos." Each title in the "Eskimos" box is a little SUBJECT MATTER in itself. Can you add one more division to "Eskimos"—one *more* smaller SUBJECT MATTER? Write it in the empty box.

---

15. So it will help in comprehending our paragraph if we decide on *the particular part* of the Eskimo world that the pararaph concentrates on. That particular part is, of course, the "taboo" in the Eskimo's life. So now our SM can be shown more precisely:

▶ Look at Part 15. The area taken up by "taboo" is a part of the large area taken up by "Eskimos." "Taboo" is the *specific* SUBJECT MATTER.

13.

What the paragraph is about is called the SUBJECT MATTER of the paragraph.

white trappers

Indians | *(SM)* ESKIMOS | wolves

seals

14. Directions: Write one more smaller subject matter for "Eskimos."

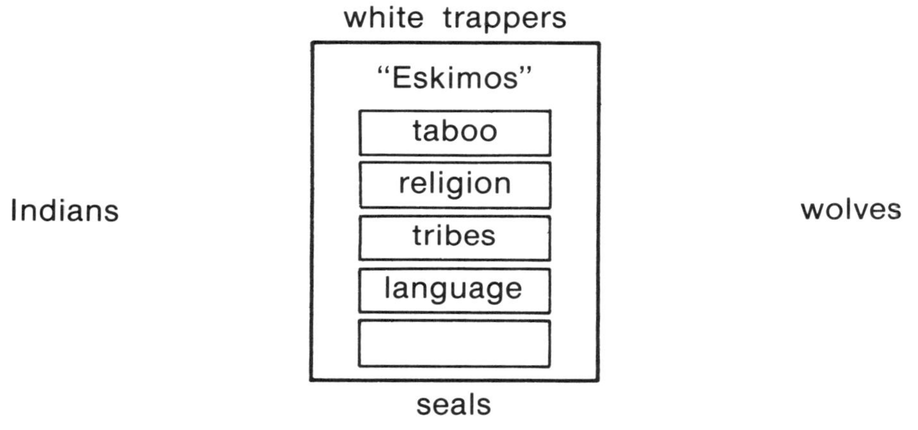

15.

Paragraph 11 concentrates on the "taboo" in the Eskimo's life. "Taboo" is the specific SUBJECT MATTER.

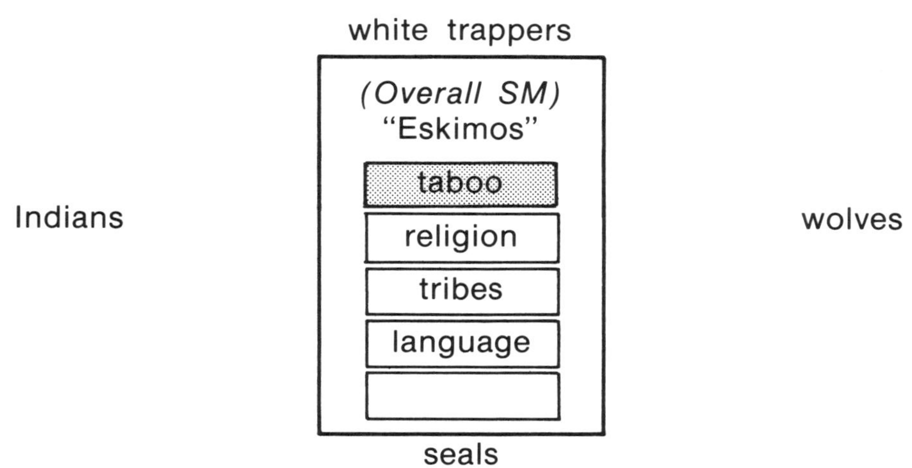

16.

So, when you have spotted the DETAILS, and are starting to look for the SM, first ask yourself:

"What is the *overall* SUBJECT MATTER?" Second, ask yourself:

"What division, what phase, what part, of the overall SM is the paragraph really concentrating on?"

► To make this idea crystal clear, do the exercise in Part 16. Read the paragraph. Then answer questions 1 and 2.

Answers: 1. The overall Subject Matter is "jockeys."
2. The specific Subject Matter is "the pay of jockeys," or "the earnings of jockeys," or "jockey's pay," etc.

The G and the D's

Once you have the SM of the paragraph clear in your mind, it's easier to go to the next step — finding the G.

If you know that the passage is about "the pay of jockeys," you can then ask the question:

"What does the author say about the "pay of jockeys?"

► Look in the paragraph now at the DETAIL. What does the DETAIL show about the "pay of jockeys"? That is question 3. Write your answer on the line.

Answer: Jockeys earn large sums.

► Question 4 is, "What is the GENERAL STATEMENT?" Put the SM together with the D, and you get the G. Write your answer.

Answer: Our G is: "Jockeys are well paid."

17.

The "G"

We said before that the G is related to—or based on—the D's in "a certain way."

Let's start by saying that to find the G takes thought. It's not easy. It's not "cut-and-dried." The only way to become good at this part of comprehension is to practice doing it. That's why you will find 66 passages to practice on after this Part One.

If you are going to be looking for the G (and what could be more important in reading?), it helps to understand what kind of thinking is called for on your part when you do it.

16.

Directions: Read this paragraph. Answer questions 1 and 2.

Jockeys are well paid. A jockey keeps about 10% of the money his horses win. Jacinto Vasquez, a five-foot-three comer, has ridden horses to $7,000,000 in wins in the last eight years. Which means he earned almost $100,000 a year.

1. What is the overall SUBJECT MATTER?

____

2. What is the specific SUBJECT MATTER?

____

3. What does the DETAIL show about the "pay of jockeys"?

____

4. What is the GENERAL STATEMENT?

____

17.

(cont'd) We said that the G (general statement) is based on the D's (details). The DETAILS, we said, give "body" to the G — they prove it, clarify it, make it more interesting.

But what does the G *do* for the paragraph?

The G puts a "handle" on the paragraph. It makes it easier to remember by wrapping up all the details in one main thought. It makes it easier and faster to talk about the paragraph. It's like a shorthand symbol — it "sums up" the paragraph in just one sentence. The G is, if you get down to it, what the author is really trying to say.

► For example, look at Part 17. Read these sentences. What do they have in common? What is the author trying to say? Write your answer in one sentence.

Answer: "She's beautiful."

Now how did you jump to the G so fast?

You read each D and began to see THE THOUGHT THAT WAS COMMON TO EACH D: each D involved an element of beauty. You pulled out the thing that each sentence had in common with the other sentences—*the common element*—and that gave you the G.

18.

► Look at Part 18. What do all these items have in common? Where are they all usually found? Write your answer.

Answer: All these items are found in **the bathroom**.

19.

► In Part 19 all of the items listed have to do with food. But some of them have one part of a meal in common. Check all the items that have to do with just one part of a meal. Then tell what part of a meal they involve.

Answer: Tomato, lettuce, salad dressing, cucumber, parsley, and salad bowl. The checked items all have to do with the salad.

---

17. Directions: Read these sentences. What do they have in common? What is the author trying to say? Write your answer in one sentence.

"She's got thick, glossy-black hair."

"She's got a perfect figure."

"She has eyes like deep pools."

"Her skin is soft and smooth."

The "G" is: ______________________________

---

18. Directions: What do all these items have in common? Where are they usually found?

toothbrush | soap
shampoo | towels
pills | washcloths

All these items are found in the ______________________.

---

19. Directions: Check all the items that have to do with just one part of a meal.

____ tomato | ____ oatmeal
____ steak | ____ cucumber
____ fork | ____ pan
____ lettuce | ____ parsley
____ salad dressing | ____ salad bowl

The checked items have to do with the ______________.

20.

▶ Look at Part 20. Here is a series of statements that people made to a reporter. Name the emotion that is common to all their statements. Then put that emotion into a sentence so that it makes a G-statement.

Answer: (a) The common emotion in these details is fear.

(b) The G-statement is: All these people are afraid.

So, to come up with a "G" — with a GENERAL STATEMENT — you have to put all the D's together and then look at them to see what they have in common. And then you have to state this common element in a simple, straightforward declarative sentence that makes a statement about the SUBJECT MATTER.

21.

▶ Look at Part 21. Here's a bit more practice on G-thinking. Read this paragraph and fill in the G-statement about the facts given.

Answer: The books in our library are in alphabetical order.

22.

▶ Read Part 22 and make a G-statement about the facts given.

Answer: Playing cards were popular in every country (in Europe).

23.

Now let's generalize about some details in a typical passage from history. The author of the passage in Part 23 is writing about Americans. Each of the details is really about the same thought. A common thread runs through all these details.

▶ Make a G-statement for the paragraph.

Answer: Americans will fight oppressors; (or)

Americans will fight for their freedom; (or)

Americans will stand up and fight would-be aggressors (enemies).

24.

There are just a few more hints about how to nail the G, and then you'll be ready to try your hand at the passages in Part Two.

In the paragraphs you have just worked with, the G itself was not stated in words. The D's were there, but the G was not in any one particular sentence.

20. These paragraphs give you practice in writing GENERAL STATEMENTS. Follow the directions of your instructor.

(1) "I'm afraid to walk down the street at night," the young man said, spreading his hands in a gesture of disbelief. (2) "You look at every car that passes and you don't know if somebody will shoot at you," said a cop. (3) An elderly woman has twice been on a bus that was attacked. She goes shopping less often.

(a) The common emotion in these details is ____________.

(b) The G-statement is: ______________________________.

21.

In our library books by authors whose names begin with "A" are placed on the first shelf you come to. After them we put the books by authors whose names begin with "B." Then we place the "C" authors after them. Then come the "D" authors. The "Z" authors are placed at the end of the last shelves.

A G-statement about the D's would be:

____

22.

As far back as 1379, playing cards were known in Italy. Instead of Hearts, Diamonds, Spades, and Clubs, the Italians used Cups, Coins, Swords, and Batons. Cards were used by the Spaniards. They used the same suits as the Italians, but the pictures on the cards were simpler. Germany, too, saw playing cards. In fact, the Germans made sets of cards for selling to other countries. The Swiss, French, and even the gypsies all played with cards.

A general statement (G) about playing cards would be:

____

23.

England wanted to tell the colonies what to do. She did so by taxing the Americans. The Americans wouldn't sit still for English taxes and fought the War of 1776. In 1812 the English tried to push our seamen around. They took them off U.S. ships and sent them to prison. We fought the War of 1812. We fought the Barbary pirates who were a threat to our freedom of the seas. And when France wanted to invade New York City by sea, we built Fort John Jay in New York harbor. The French, by the way, never attacked.

The G-statement is: ______________________________.

24.

(cont'd)

Usually, however, the author *will* put the G into a definite sentence. He may put the G in the *first* sentence. He may put it in the *last* sentence. Or he may write it somewhere in the *middle* of the paragraph. There's no one place the G has to be.

On the other hand, there are times when the author doesn't make it that easy. He wants you to think about the passage and come up with the G in your own words. When the G isn't stated in the paragraph, we call it an "IMPLIED" G.

But no matter how a G is stated, or where it's put, the steps in finding it are the same.

....

First, find the DETAILS.

Then find the *overall* SUBJECT MATTER.

Then decide what phase of the *overall* SUBJECT MATTER the paragraph is really about — the *specific* SUBJECT MATTER.

And finally, ask yourself what the DETAILS are telling you about the *specific* SUBJECT MATTER.

....

One more thought:

You may have noticed that we've been using the words *paragraph* and *passages* interchangeably in the last few pages of these instructions. A passage could be just one paragraph. Usually, it's a few paragraphs, all with the same SM.

Now, the basic ideas — concepts — you have been working with *are* basic. They apply to the sentence. They apply to the paragraph. And they apply to the passage. Short or long, when a person writes, it's got to be *about* something (SM), it's got to *say* something about the subject (G), and it should *back up* that statement (D's).

And finally:

These ideas, this approach to reading, may be a bit new to you. *You need not have mastered them at this point.* You probably need more practice. Only after you have worked with these ideas for a while will you really come to make them yours. It takes time. But as you do passage after passage, and answer question after question, your reading will improve.

Because you are *thinking* as you read.

PART TWO:

DOING IT

PASSAGES 1 to 66
WITH QUESTIONS

1

Sometimes fear pays off. At least it does for Dean Watson, a man who has a one-horse stable in Quebec, Canada. His horse, Charon, has won six races for Watson and earned him $93,000 last year.

"Charon," Watson explained, "is afraid of the other horses. When he finds them all around him at the start of a race, he tries very hard to get away from them. He finds it easiest to get away by getting out in front."

PASSAGE 1 QUESTIONS

Directions: If the sentence is true, circle **True**. If the sentence is false, circle **False**.

(D) **1.** Dean Watson owns only one horse. True False

(D) **2.** The horse, Charon, didn't win much last year. True False

(D) **3.** Charon likes to be with other horses. True False

(SM) **4.** The passage is mainly about a man named Dean Watson. True False

Directions: Circle the letter of the choice that best completes the thought below.

(G) **5.** Charon wins because

A. he runs in many races.
B. he finds it easy to win.
C. he is afraid of other horses.
D. he feels crowded at the start of a race.

Directions: Answer these questions. Write your answer on the line after the question.

(SM) **6.** What would be a good title for Passage 1?

____

(G) **7.** What makes Charon a winner?

____

(D) **8.** Why does Charon get out in front of the other horses?

____

2

Could an eagle carry off a human baby? Ever since the story of Sinbad the Sailor we've heard tales of human young being carried off by big birds. Sinbad, so the story goes, was carried off by the Roc. The Roc—a huge bird—took Sinbad in his beak and flew him off to his nest in the mountains.

Sinbad and the Roc were only imaginary. But what about eagles? Can an eagle lift a baby?

Two scientists wanted to find out. They climbed up into the high mountains and captured a golden eagle. They tied an eight-pound weight to its neck. Eight pounds, they felt, was about the right weight for a very young baby. Then they let the eagle loose. The eagle couldn't get off the ground!

PASSAGE 2 QUESTIONS

Directions: Circle **True** or **False** for each sentence.

(D) **1.** The Roc was a real bird that lived long ago. It could lift people. True False

(D) **2.** Stories have been told of human babies being carried off by birds. We don't know if these stories are true. True False

Directions: Which choice best completes the thought? Circle the letter.

(SM) **3.** This passage is about

A. eagles.
B. the lifting power of eagles.
C. two scientists.
D. Sinbad the Sailor.

Directions: Answer these questions.

(D) **4.** What did the scientists tie to the eagle's neck? ____________________

(G) **5.** What is the "point" (the General Statement) of Passage 2?

____

(D) **6.** Why do you think your answer to question 5 is correct?

____

3

Do you slurp soup? Do you pop bubble gum? If you do, your habits won't help you win friends—but they're fun. But how about knuckle-popping? Not only does this hobby give people around you the "willies," but cracking knuckles can lead to monster knuckles, and maybe—to arthritis.

At least, most people think knuckle-popping is bad. Well, there's no doubt that the people who have to listen to knuckles being snapped can't stand the sound. But how bad is it for the knuckle-popper?

A doctor has looked into this indoor sport. He says it's not harmful. Dr. Robert L. Swezey of UCLA found that his son was cracking his knuckles. And the kid's grandmother thought it was terrible. So Dr. Swezey went to a home for the aged. He studied the knuckles of old people there. Only one out of fifteen old people who said they cracked their knuckles all their lives had anything wrong with their finger joints. Also, five out of twelve women who *never* cracked their knuckles had trouble with their joints. So, if you want to go on popping your knuckles, Dr. Swezey says it's O.K. Even if his son's grandma still doesn't like it.

PASSAGE 3 QUESTIONS

Directions: Answer these questions. Write your answer on the line after the question.

(D) **1.** When Dr. Swezey went to the old-age-home, what did he find out about old people who had cracked their knuckles?

____

(D) **2.** What did he find out about old people who had never cracked their knuckles?

____

Directions: Circle the letter of the choice that best completes each thought below.

(D) **3.** People who hear others cracking their knuckles

A. are bothered.
B. don't notice the sound.
C. start to crack their own knuckles.
D. feel it's as bad as slurping soup.

(SM) **4.** This passage is about

A. knuckle-popping.
B. arthritis.
C. people in old-age-homes.
D. Dr. Swezey's son.

Directions: Answer this question.

(G) **5.** What is Dr. Swezey's idea about knuckle-popping?

____

Directions: Which choice best completes the thought? Circle the letter.

(SIG) **6.** If you pop your knuckles, Dr. Swezey thinks you should

A. go on doing it.
B. stop at once.
C. avoid people who do it.
D. not do it around your friends.

4

The Greeks of olden times told many stories. Some of these stories seem strangely up-to-date. One of the stories was about Milo of Crotona. Milo was a young shepherd. He had an idea that he wanted to become as strong as Hercules. So, when a baby ox was born to his herd, he hit on a plan. He made up his mind to lift the ox every day. Each day the ox grew bigger. Each day Milo lifted him. Finally the ox was full-grown. And Milo was able to lift him. . . . Is there a full-grown "ox" you want to lift someday? Take a hint from Milo. Start when it's young and small—and lift it every day.

PASSAGE 4 QUESTIONS

Directions: Answer these questions. Write your answers on the lines.

(D) **1.** The story of Milo is an old one. Why does the writer tell it now?

____

(D) **2.** Why did Milo lift the ox?

____

(D) **3.** How strong did Milo get?

____

(D) **4.** How often did he lift the ox?

____

(SM) **5.** What does the writer mean by the words *a full-grown "ox"*?

____

(SM) **6.** What is the writer really writing about?

____

(G) **7.** What does the writer try to prove with Milo's story?

____

(SIG) **8.** What advice does the passage give you about doing big things?

____

5

It's hard to hurt a shark. One man hooked a spinner shark. It leaped and whirled on the line. After twenty minutes he got it boatside. The shark was small—under four feet long. But it had nice jaws, and the fisherman wanted a pair of shark jaws. He brought out his .22 and put four shots neatly through the rear of the shark's head. This was the right spot for a kill. The shark lay still. Then it came to life. It threw the hook and swam away.

The man put out more bait and pulled in seven more sharks. He was about to call it a day. Just then, another shark took off with his line. The thing fought and fought. When he got it alongside, the man saw a nice pair of jaws—and four neat red holes in the shark's head.

Sharks have been known to live with a half dozen shots from a rifle. They have taken a close-up blast from a 12-gauge shotgun. They have shrugged off a spray of broadhead hunting arrows. A bayonet on a pole, thrust into the shark's throat, has failed to slow it down. No wonder the shark is called the monster fish.

PASSAGE 5 QUESTIONS

Directions: If the sentence is true, circle **True**. If the sentence is false, circle **False**.

(D) **1.** The spinner did not seem to be hurt by four bullets in his head. True False

(D) **2.** Sharks seem to be hurt more by arrows than by bullets or bayonets. True False

Directions: Complete each sentence.

(SM) **3.** The purpose of this passage is to explain

____

(G) **4.** This passage proves that it's hard to hurt a shark. By proving this, it shows why sharks

____

6

The monster fish are old. And strange. They were on the earth millions of years before man. In their cold eyes lurks the grimness of the ancient world. Aside from their jaws, they have no bones. Their spinal cords are housed only in cartilage, not bone. Unlike other fish, sharks cannot pump water through their gills. So, to get oxygen they must move all the time. They have a super sense of smell. Some shark men think they can track prey by smell. They say sharks wag their heads from side to side in the water. Then they follow the side that has the strongest smell.

The monsters are strong. Shark experts put the force of a shark's bite at 18 tons per square inch. A Doberman's bite is 215 pounds per square inch. A shark's strength is out of this world. Not long ago, men on the pier at Palm Beach had trouble with a monster. He would come along, swallow their baits, and strip the lines from the reels. The men fixed a fat rope and a chain leader with a hand-forged hook to some bait. They lashed the rope to the pier rail. In a short while, something took the bait, and swam away with rope, chain leader, hook, and twenty feet of rail.

PASSAGE 6 QUESTIONS

Directions: If the sentence is true, circle **True**. If the sentence is false, circle **False**.

(D) **1.** Sharks are an older life-form than men. True False

(D) **2.** All of a shark's skeleton is not bone, but cartilage. True False

(D) **3.** Sharks breathe in the same way that other fish do. True False

(D) **4.** It is a fact that a shark can track prey in the water by noting which side of its head is getting the stronger smell. True False

(D) **5.** A shark may weigh up to 1,800 pounds. A shark this heavy could apply up to his full weight in pressure per square inch on something he might bite. True False

Directions: Complete each sentence.

(SM) **6.** Paragraph 2 of this passage deals with the ______________ of sharks.

(G) **7.** As far as their history goes, sharks, as a type of animal, are very

____

(D) **8.** The skeletons of sharks are made up mostly of ________________ .

(D) **9.** To breathe, sharks must ______________________________ all the time.

(D) **10.** As far as power goes, sharks are among the ____________________ of animals.

Directions: Circle the letter of the choice that best completes the thought below.

(C) **11.** When a shark sleeps, the way it breathes is

A. to move its head from side to side.
B. to move through the water slowly.
C. to sleep just a few minutes, then wake and move.
D. not explained in the passage.

7

You can hook a shark. You can get it boatside. But can you land it? The first rule is: never take a live monster into a boat. If you hold any type of monster by the tail, even a small one, watch out. He can whip around and take your hand off. Then he'll drop back into the water with your hand in his mouth and swim away.

A full-grown thresher shark is a really bad actor. He uses his tail as a secret weapon. On a 14 or 16-foot thresher, the tail may form a whip about the same length. One man hooked a big thresher off the Carolina coast. He brought the monster boatside. His partner leaned over the gunwale to take a look. Up came the whip out of the water. It caught the man under the chin and took off his head. The man's head fell into the water and his body slumped to the deck.

Fishermen have had plenty of trouble landing sharks. You can club a tuna. But a shark? Clubbing one just makes it mad.

Two fishermen out in a boat one afternoon wished that they had done just that to a hammerhead they spotted. The monster was scaring away other fish. They threw a lit stick of T.N.T. into the water. The monster swallowed it. Then he swam under the boat. BOOOOM! The men had twelve leaks in their boat. It sank as they reached the dock.

The best some fishermen can think of is to tow the shark backwards for two or three hours. Others tie him to a ginpole. They let him hang down till he dies from lack of oxygen. But there are fishermen who claim that the only sure way to finish a shark is to hold a machine gun to his head and pull the trigger.

PASSAGE 7 QUESTIONS

Directions: Answer this question. Write your answer on the line after the question.

(D) **1.** What do the words "just that" in paragraph No. 4 go back to?

____

Directions: Circle the letter of the choice that best completes each thought below.

(D) **2.** One rule for landing sharks is

A. take only small sharks into your boat.
B. if you take a shark into your boat, keep your hands away from his mouth.
C. never take a live shark into your boat.
D. never take one into your boat.

(D) **3.** A thresher shark

A. is small but deadly.
B. has a tail about 7 1/3 feet long.
C. uses his tail as a weapon.
D. puts on a show of being deadly.

(SM) **4.** The passage is mainly about

A. landing sharks after they have been hooked.
B. rules for catching sharks.
C. people who have had trouble catching sharks.
D. why sharks are more dangerous than tuna.

(G) **5.** The passage shows that

A. fishermen agree about the best way to land a shark.
B. landing a shark is difficult.
C. you can land a shark if you follow certain rules.
D. none of the above is true.

(C) **6.** Passages 5, 6, and 7 on sharks

A. never really explain why fishermen hunt sharks.
B. show that fishing for sharks needs no special training.
C. show that sharks, unlike most other animals, "start trouble" with men, rather than the other way around.
D. show that because of its danger, shark-fishing is losing its lure for fishermen.

8

Bobby Steiner, king of the bull rings, was talking to a reporter the other day about rodeos. "There's a lot of mental strain just *getting* to 120 rodeos in a year," Steiner said. "But what you do before or after the rodeo doesn't matter. It's the eight seconds you have on the bull that counts."

"In eight seconds a bull can turn 30 times. A good bull not only bucks, he spins. And we're getting better and better bulls. So, there's a fear. Well, not really a fear. But you get worked up a few days before. When you get up on them, you try to ease your way down. No, I don't try to calm them. You can't do much with a bull."

"Bulls by nature come after a cowboy. A bull like Mighty Mouse, or Double Ought, weighs about 1700 pounds. A guy like me, I weigh 150 pounds. I could get crushed. I've been stepped on. I've seen horns go through guys. But when I'm out there and the chute opens, there's not much on my mind. It's all a blur."

The payoff? Bobby Steiner won fame and fortune riding bulls. In one year he won $29,099 for the sixteen minutes he spent on their backs. "That figures out to about $1756 per minute," someone said to Steiner. "Could be," he grunted. "I earned every cent."

PASSAGE 8 QUESTIONS

Directions: Circle **True** or **False** for each sentence.

(D) **1.** Bobby Steiner does a lot of traveling in a year's time. True False

(D) **2.** The most important thing in rodeo work is to get there. True False

(D) **3.** After 120 rodeos a year, Bobby doesn't feel a thing before he gets on the bull. True False

(D) **4.** Bulls seem to hate cowboys. True False

(D) **5.** Steiner tries to think clearly when he's on the bull. True False

(D) **6.** Riding bulls is easy money. True False

Directions: Complete each sentence.

(SM) **7.** This passage is mostly about ______________________________

(G) **8.** The main thing Bobby Steiner is telling us about his work is that

____

(G) **9.** Three things are true about Bobby Steiner, king of the bull rings. They are:

A. He earns his money the hard way.
B. He likes bulls like Mighty Mouse and Double Ought.
C. He finds it a chore to get to rodeos.
D. He feels tense before a rodeo.

9

Farmer Jones was known to be stingy. He met the local vet in front of the courthouse. Here was his chance. He could get some free advice.

"Doc," he said, "I've got a peculiar horse. Sometimes he walks normal. Other times he limps. What should I do?"

The vet told him, "Next time he walks normal, sell him!"

PASSAGE 9 QUESTIONS

Directions: Which choice best completes each thought? Circle the letter.

(D) **1.** Farmer Jones asked the vet

A. to meet him in front of the courthouse.
B. to tell him how to get rid of his horse.
C. how he could cure his horse.
D. to look at his horse and tell him what was wrong.

(D) **2.** The vet

A. answered Farmer Jones's question.
B. pulled a "switch" on Farmer Jones.
C. avoided giving Farmer Jones advice.
D. wasn't helpful to Farmer Jones.

(SM) **3.** This story is about what happened to a

A. courthouse.
B. stingy farmer.
C. animal doctor.
D. horse.

(G) **4.** The point of this story is that Farmer Jones

A. was put down by the vet.
B. was helped out of a tight situation.
C. should have let well enough alone.
D. got the better of the vet.

10

In the days when the world was young, life was hard. It was hard to make a living. It was hard to raise crops. There was little rain—or too much. It was hard to keep goats and sheep. Animals grew sick. They got lost. There was war all the time.

The wise men of those days thought long about the life of man. They put their thoughts into stories. One of these stories has been told and retold over the years. It is the story of Joseph and his brothers.

Joseph was seventeen when we first meet him. He was the son of Jacob's old age. Jacob loved Joseph more than his other sons. He made Joseph a coat. The coat had long sleeves and many colors.

When they saw the coat of many colors, Joseph's brothers knew that their father loved him best. So they hated him. They spoke harshly to him.

Now Joseph had a dream. He told it to his brothers. "Listen," he said, "to this dream I have had. We were binding bunches of grain. My sheaf rose up and stood upright. Then I saw your sheaves gather round and bow to my sheaf."

"So you want to be king over us," his brothers said. His brothers hated him still more.

Then Joseph had another dream. He told this dream to his father and his brothers. "I thought," said Joseph, "that I saw the sun, the moon, and eleven stars bow down to me."

His father scolded him. "A fine dream to have. Are all of us then, myself, your mother, and all your brothers to bow down to the ground before you?"

PASSAGE 10 QUESTIONS

Directions: Circle **True** or **False** for each sentence.

(D) **1.** Long ago, it was hard to raise crops, but it was easy to keep goats and sheep. True False

(D) **2.** Joseph was younger than his brothers. True False

(D) **3.** His brothers hated Joseph because he had a coat of many colors. True False

This passage is a story. Usually a story has a plot—things happen. They usually happen to people. If you know about the story of Joseph, you know he was the main person (character) in the story—the "hero." The hero has to struggle against forces in the place he lives, or against people, or both. Here Joseph's struggle (it's called a "conflict") begins early. It is the conflict of the hero with forces or people against him, that makes a story interesting.

Directions: Answer each question. Write the paragraph numbers on the line after the question.

(SM) **4.** Which paragraph or paragraphs tell how the story of Joseph came to be written? ____________

(SM) **5.** Which paragraph or paragraphs set up the conflict? ____________

(SM) **6.** Which paragraphs show the conflict getting sharper? ____________

Directions: Which choice best completes each thought? Circle the letter.

(G) **7.** The conflict in this story is between

A. Joseph and his father.
B. Joseph and Nature.
C. Joseph and his brothers.
D. Joseph and himself.

(D) **8.** Joseph's first dream seemed to mean that

A. Joseph and his brothers were good at farming.
B. the bunches of grain have a life of their own.
C. his brothers wanted him to rule.
D. Joseph would have power over his brothers.

Directions: Answer this question. Write your answer on the line.

(C) **9.** Can you think of a reason why Joseph has had the two dreams he tells of?

____

11

Joseph's brothers went to pasture their flocks in the valley of Hebron. Jacob sent Joseph to see how his brothers were doing.

When his brothers saw Joseph coming, they made a plot to get rid of him. "Here comes the man of dreams," they said to one another. "Come, let us kill him."

But Reuben, one of the brothers, said, "After all, he is of our flesh. Let us throw him into a pit, but not kill him." Reuben thought that this would give him a chance to save his brother.

Looking up, they saw a caravan. The camels were loaded with gum, balsam, and resin. The caravan was going to Egypt. So the brothers took Joseph out of the pit. They took off his coat, and sold him.

The brothers took the coat and put goat's blood on it. Then they brought it to their father. "Look, a wild beast has killed Joseph." Joseph's father wept for his son. He put a sack on his body. He mourned for Joseph. His sons and daughters came to comfort him. But he would not be comforted.

PASSAGE 11 QUESTIONS

Directions: Complete these questions.

(D) **1.** Joseph went to where his brothers were pasturing flocks because

____

(D) **2.** His brothers planned to kill Joseph because

____

(D) **3.** Reuben pleaded for mercy for Joseph because

____

(D) **4.** The brothers harmed Joseph by

____

(D) **5.** The brothers put goat's blood on Joseph's coat because

____

(SM) **6.** This second part of the Joseph story is mainly about

____

Directions: Circle the letter of the choice that best completes the thought below.

(G) **7.** The point of this part of the story is that the brothers

A. preserved Joseph's life.
B. wronged Joseph.
C. left him in a well.
D. wanted his coat of many colors.

12

Meanwhile, the men of the caravan sold Joseph to Potiphar, a top man in Pharaoh's army. But God was with Joseph. All that Potiphar told him to do, Joseph did well. Whatever he turned his hand to came out well. So Potiphar made Joseph his personal aide. He put Joseph in charge of his household. Joseph ran everything. Potiphar had an easy life.

Potiphar's wife liked Joseph's looks. Joseph was well-built and handsome. She wanted Joseph to love her. Joseph refused.

"Look," he told Potiphar's wife, "my master has put me in charge. I guard all the things he owns. You are his wife. How could I do anything to betray his trust?"

One day Joseph came to the house. There were no servants indoors. Potiphar's wife caught hold of his tunic and said, "Stay with me." He left his tunic and ran out of the house. "Look at this," she said. "See how the Hebrew insults us. He came to show his love for me, but I screamed."

PASSAGE 12 QUESTIONS

Directions: Answer these questions. Write your answer on the line after the question.

(D) **1.** Why did Joseph do well in Potiphar's service?

____

(D) **2.** Why wouldn't Joseph love Potiphar's wife?

____

(D) **3.** Why did Potiphar's wife accuse Joseph?

____

Directions: Circle the letter of the choice that best completes each thought below.

(SM) **4.** In this part of the story Joseph

A. meets another crisis in his life.
B. completely overcomes his problems.
C. betrays his trust.
D. handles everything perfectly.

(G) **5.** The saying that best sums up this part of the Joseph story might be

A. "Hell hath no fury like a woman scorned."
B. "Out of the frying pan into the fire."
C. "You can't keep a good man down."
D. "Honesty is the best policy."

13

1. When Potiphar heard his wife's story, he was mad. He sent Joseph to jail. Joseph was put where the Pharaoh's prisoners were kept.

In jail God was with Joseph. The chief jailer liked him. He put Joseph in charge of the other prisoners. Everything in the jail worked fine.

It so happened that the Pharaoh's cupbearer and chief baker were also in jail. They had both done something that Pharaoh didn't like. The jailer asked Joseph to care for them.

---

2. Now both of these men had dreams the same night. When Joseph saw them in the morning, they looked gloomy. "Why these black faces?" asked Joseph.

"Because we have had dreams. There is no one here to tell us what the dreams mean."

Joseph said, "Come, tell me."

---

3. The chief cupbearer said, "In my dream I saw a vine in front of me. On the vine were three branches. Each branch budded. Then the buds had blossoms. Then the blossoms bore clusters of grapes. I had Pharaoh's cup in my hand. I picked the grapes. I put them in Pharaoh's cup. I put the cup in Pharaoh's hand."

"Here is what your dream means," said Joseph. "The three branches are three days. In three days Pharaoh will let you go free. He will put you back in your place. Then you will hand Pharaoh his cup. When you go back, please say a good word to Pharaoh about me. I want to be free."

---

4. The chief baker saw that Joseph gave a good meaning. So he told his dream: "There were three trays of Pharaoh's cakes on my head. But the birds ate the cakes off the trays."

Joseph gave him this answer: "The three trays are three days. In another three days Pharaoh will take you out of this jail, and hang you. The birds will eat the flesh off your bones."

---

5. And so it went. The third day was Pharaoh's birthday. He put the chief cupbearer in his place to hand him his cup. But he hanged the chief baker. It was as Joseph said. But the cupbearer did not speak for Joseph. He forgot him.

PASSAGE 13 QUESTIONS

Directions: Complete these sentences.

(D) **1.** Joseph was put in charge of the other prisoners because

____

(D) **2.** Joseph helped Pharaoh's cupbearer by

____

(D) **3.** The cupbearer was put in his place by Pharaoh. The chief baker was hanged. So the meaning Joseph gave to their dreams was

____

Directions: Give a title to each section.

(SM) **4.** Section 1: A good title for this section would be:

____

Section 2: ______________________________

Section 3: ______________________________

Section 4: ______________________________

Section 5: ______________________________

Directions: Answer this question.

(G) **5.** Later on, in the next part of the Joseph story, Joseph will give a correct meaning to Pharaoh's dream. What do you think is the purpose of the passage you have just read?

____

____

14

Two years later, Pharaoh had a dream. He was standing by the Nile. There, coming up from the Nile, were seven cows. The cows were fat and sleek. They began to feed among the plants at the river's edge. Then seven other cows, lean and ugly, came up from the river. The ugly cows ate the sleek and fat cows. Then Pharaoh awoke.

He fell asleep and dreamed a second time. There, growing on one stalk, were seven ears of corn. Each ear was full and ripe. Then there grew seven other ears of corn. These ears looked scanty and burned. The scanty ears swallowed the full and ripe ears of corn. Then Pharaoh awoke.

That morning Pharaoh called all his wise men to him. Pharaoh told his dream. But none could say what it meant. Then the chief cupbearer spoke. "There was a young Hebrew with us in jail. He interpreted our dreams. And it turned out as he had said."

Pharaoh had Joseph come before him. Joseph was taken from the jail. He shaved, and put on clean clothing.

Pharaoh spoke to Joseph, "I have had a dream. No one can interpret it. I have heard it said of you that you can interpret."

Joseph said, "I do not count. It is God who will give Pharaoh a good answer."

So Pharaoh told Joseph his dreams. "Pharaoh's dreams are one and the same," said Joseph. "God has revealed to Pharaoh what He will do. The seven fine cows are seven good years. The seven lean cows are seven lean years. And the same for the seven ripe ears and the seven poor ears of corn."

"Seven years of plenty are coming to Egypt. Then seven years of famine will come. The land will be bare of grain. The reason the dream came twice is because God has decided."

"Pharaoh should now choose a wise man to govern the land of Egypt. One fifth of all the grain should be taken and stored. The food shall be stored in Pharaoh's name. The food will serve as a reserve in the seven lean years."

Then Pharaoh said, "Seeing that God has made you know this, you shall be the man. All my people shall obey your orders. Only I will be above you. I hereby make you governor of Egypt." Pharaoh took his ring. He put it on Joseph's finger. He clothed Joseph in fine linen. He put a gold chain around his neck. He made him ride in his best chariot. Riders rode before Joseph crying, "Make way!" And Pharaoh gave Joseph Asenath, daughter of a priest of Egypt, for his wife.

PASSAGE 14 QUESTIONS

Directions: Which choice best completes each thought? Circle the letter.

(D) **1.** Joseph's special gift was that he

A. got on well with people.
B. was a Hebrew.
C. could tell what dreams meant.
D. knew about cows and corn.

(D) **2.** Joseph got to the Pharaoh's ear because

A. the Pharaoh had heard about him.
B. the cupbearer recommended him.
C. he had been in jail for two years.
D. Pharaoh had no wise men.

(D) **3.** Joseph felt that

A. God spoke through him.
B. the dream of Pharaoh was easy to interpret.
C. he was, himself, a wise man.
D. Pharaoh had dreamt two different dreams: one about the fat years and one about the lean years.

Directions: This story breaks up into four parts.

1. Pharaoh's dreams
2. A challenge for Joseph
3. A successful meeting of the challenge
4. Joseph's victory

(SM) **4.** Draw **three** lines across the passage from the left to the right margin to show where Parts 1, 2, 3, and 4 begin and end. Number the sections.

Directions: Answer these questions.

(G) **5.** What is the most important thing that happens to Joseph in this part of the story? ______________________________

(C) **6.** This story from the Bible has been read by many, many people over thousands of years. Why do you think its plot is so interesting to people? ______________________________

15

1. Joseph was now thirty years old. The seven fat years came. Joseph saw to it that part of the grain was stored in each town. The grain was like the sand. There was so much that it was beyond counting.

2. After the seven fat years came the seven lean years. There was no food all over the world. First the Egyptians came to Joseph to buy grain. Then the people from other lands beyond Egypt came to buy.

3. In the land of Canaan Joseph's brothers were without food. "Why are you standing there looking at each other?" Jacob, Joseph's father, asked his sons. "I hear that there is grain for sale in the land of Goshen (Egypt). Go down and buy grain, that we may live."

4. So the brothers went to Egypt to buy grain. They left Benjamin, the youngest brother, with Jacob. "Nothing must happen to my youngest," said the father.

5. When they came to Joseph, they did not know him. But Joseph knew his brothers. "Where have you come from?" he asked. "From the land of Canaan, to buy grain." "You are spies," Joseph said. "You have come to spy out the country's weak points." "No, my lord," they said, "we are honest men. We have come to buy grain. Your servants are twelve brothers. The youngest is with our father. The twelfth brother is no more." "Well, if you are honest, bring me the youngest. If he does not come to me, then you have failed the test. You will die."

6. The brothers left one brother, Simeon, as hostage. Joseph gave them some sacks of grain to take back to their father. But he had his servants put gold pieces in the sacks. It was another test.

7. The first night on their trip home the brothers stopped to make camp. Then they found the gold. They were worried that Joseph would think they had stolen it.

8. When they came to their father's house, they told him the story. "Take Benjamin to the lord," Jacob said, "take double the money back to show that you are not thieves."

9. When Joseph saw Benjamin with his brothers, he went aside and wept. He could no longer treat his brothers harshly. So he said to his servants, "Leave me." Then he said, "I am Joseph. I am lord over Egypt under only Pharaoh. Do not feel badly that you sold me into slavery. God has seen to it that I would save you and all of Jacob's people. He kissed his brothers. He had Benjamin sit beside him. He made a feast for his brothers. Joseph gave Benjamin food from his own dish.

10. Then Joseph had his brothers go to Canaan. And all of Jacob's people, his goats, and his cattle, were brought to Egypt. They settled there in Egypt and lived good lives until Pharaoh died.

PASSAGE 15 QUESTIONS

Directions: If the sentence is true, circle **True.** If the sentence is false, circle **False.**

(D) **1.** During the seven lean years, only Egyptians had to buy food. True False

(D) **2.** When the lean years came, Joseph's brothers knew what to do. True False

(D) **3.** At the time Joseph's brothers came to Egypt, there were twelve of Jacob's sons living. True False

Directions: Answer these questions.

(D) **4.** Why do you think Joseph had gold put into the sacks of his brothers?

____

____

(SM) **5.** Which paragraph or paragraphs tell about the first test that Joseph puts to his brothers? __________

(SM) **6.** Which paragraph or paragraphs tell about the second test? __________

(SM) **7.** In which paragraph does the climax of the Joseph story come? __________

(G) **8.** What is the main thing that happens in this last part of the Joseph story? ______________________________

____

16

Indians called the small mammal O POS SUM — white beast. He's one of the best actors in the business. Hunters know that when they find an opossum, he puts on an act of being "dead." He's "playing 'possum." They can tweak his whiskers. They can twist his toes. No sign of life. The 'possum doesn't seem to be breathing. His mouth is open. His tongue hangs out. Even his heartbeat is hard to detect.

Is the opossum really asleep? Is he paralyzed?

A team of California biologists put a little 'possum on the lab table. They wired his brain. Then they "attacked" him. A dog's bark was played on a record. They grabbed the possum's neck with a pliers. He thought the dog was biting him. So he played dead. His act was good — he looked dead all right. But the machine the scientists used showed his brain to be active and alert. He was just "playing 'possum."

PASSAGE 16 QUESTIONS

Directions: Which choice best completes each thought? Circle the letter.

(D) **1.** When hunters find an opossum,

A. the opossum puts on an act to amuse them.
B. the opossum stops breathing.
C. the opossum's heart stops beating.
D. the opossum plays "dead."

(D) **2.** When the biologists got the opossum into the lab, they

A. attacked him.
B. let a dog bite him.
C. recorded his brain waves on a record.
D. made him think he was being attacked.

(D) **3.** On the lab table, the scientists found that

A. he was asleep.
B. his brain was alert.
C. he was in pain.
D. his breathing had stopped.

(SM) **4.** The passage deals mainly with

A. the opossum's size.
B. what goes on when the opossum plays dead.
C. how the opossum defeats his enemies.
D. the work of California biologists.

(G) **5.** The passage proves that

A. the 'possum is a faker.
B. the 'possum is smart.
C. the 'possum isn't fooling anybody.
D. when the opossum plays dead, he's really asleep.

17

Want to be taller? And slimmer? Take a space flight! At least that's what Dr. Story Musgrave, a doctor who was aboard Skylab 3, seems to be saying. He told the three other astronauts who were aboard Skylab 3 with him that they had grown taller since they left the earth. The men grew between one and two inches taller. And they were smaller around the chest and waist. The increase in height was caused by a shift in fluids in the men's bodies. "Without gravity," Dr. Musgrave said, "the discs in the men's spines were taking in more water, and so were getting longer. And the anti-gravity muscles in the back were not pressing the discs together, as they do on earth."

PASSAGE 17 QUESTIONS

Directions: Complete these sentences.

(D) **1.** During their space flight the men's spinal discs became ____________

(D) **2.** The reason why this happened was that ____________

____

(D) **3.** Because their anti-gravity muscles were not working, their spinal discs were not being ____________ together.

(SM) **4.** This passage is talking mostly about ____________

____

(G) **5.** If you took a space flight, the chances are that you would become

____

18

"Mame" is a play, with music, about a wonderful woman. Her friends call her "Auntie Mame." Auntie Mame is a special kind of person. She thinks for herself. She doesn't follow the crowd.

Mame's idea about life is that you should do new things every day. You should not bury yourself in the same routine. One of the songs in the show is "Open a New Window."

Auntie Mame's only living relative is a red-headed young boy, Patrick Dennis. He comes to live with Auntie Mame in New York.

With Mame's help, Patrick learns to play a bugle. He learns to dance. He meets strange people who have had adventures and who dress in odd ways. Mame takes him out of school for a long trip around the world. He visits India and Africa.

Patrick grows up to be a nice person. He is not afraid to do new and different things. He never forgets his love for Auntie Mame — she showed him how to "open new windows."

Think about your own life. Are you doing the same things today that you did a week ago? A month ago? A year ago? Perhaps we should all listen to Auntie Mame.

PASSAGE 18 QUESTIONS

Directions: Write the answers to these questions.

(D) **1.** What is the song, "Open a New Window," in praise of?

____

(D) **2.** Why does Patrick love his Auntie Mame? ______________________________

(D) **3.** Was Patrick a typical schoolboy? ______________________________

Why do you think your answer is right? ______________________________

____

(SM) **4.** What is this passage mainly about? ______________________________

(G) **5.** Why is Auntie Mame a "special kind of person"? ______________________________

____

19

Were you ever stuck with a product that didn't work out? Some people who have been buying "super-sticky" glue have been really stuck. They have had their fingers glued together. Others have had their fingers stuck to other parts of their bodies. They needed medical help.

The glue is known as "cyano-acrylic" and was made for surgeons. It's a good, all-purpose glue. It will glue anything to anything. The trouble is, it may be too good.

So if you buy "super-glue," watch out — it may really work on you!

PASSAGE 19 QUESTIONS

Directions: Write the answers to these questions.

(D) **1.** What happened to some people who used cyano-acrylic glue?

____

(D) **2.** For whom was the glue made?

____

(G) **3.** How good is the cyano-acrylic glue?

____

(SIG) **4.** What does the author suggest that you do about the glue?

____

20

If you ever skin-dive off-shore—or swim off a boat—you may meet one of the mysteries of the sea — the killer whale. Should you panic? Or should you calmly get back into your boat and take a good look at the big boy?

Go on to next page. ➤

For years little was known about the killer whale. But in the last few years scientists, fishermen, and skin divers have been putting it all together. The central fact about the killer whale is that, like man, it's a social animal.

The killers hunt as a group. Their group is called a *pod.* A tuna fisherman, Tom Mix, saw a pod feeding on a small herd of dolphins in the Southeast Pacific. Fifteen of the killers circled the dolphins. They swam fast. They always made the circle smaller. Suddenly, a killer left the circle. He swam straight through the dolphin school. As he swam he bit and chewed on anything he hit. Within minutes all the killers used the same tactic. After each strike, they would go back to the circle. This kept the dolphins trapped. The water grew red with blood. The dolphins were slower than the killers. They were confused by the hit-and-run tactics.

Killer whales aren't true whales. They are the largest of the forty kinds of dolphins. They reach about forty feet in length. They then weigh about 15,000 pounds. The early whalers named them "whale killers." Later on, the name "whale killer" was turned around.

The family set-up is very strong among the killers. A pair will give birth to a calf once every two years. The mother suckles the young calf. She protects it. From birth to death a killer stays with its pod. Each pod member protects the others.

Pod members talk to each other all the time. A killer has no vocal cords. The sounds it makes come from its blowhole. The blowhole is in the center of its forehead. It makes a kind of whistle. The whistle can act as a distress call. Each killer's sound is unique. So the whistle also serves to tell who is sending the signal. Killers also make clicks and "click trains" when talking.

A killer who is sending out a signal is given total silence by the pod. When the killer has finished his talking, then another one will talk. The only pod-member who can "talk-over" the signal is the pod leader.

Strangely, killers never hurt man. That is, unless man hurts the killer first. That is why marinelands all over the world feature killer whales. In the marineland, the killers learn fast. A newly taken killer is put in with the trained animals. Soon he has picked up all the tricks. But the men who show the killers must keep ahead of them. The animals soon get bored with the same tricks, and invent new tricks of their own!

PASSAGE 20 QUESTIONS

Directions: Which choice best completes each thought? Circle the letter.

(D) **1.** A killer whale, when born,

A. leaves its mother and swims with the pod.
B. is fed by its mother.
C. lives by eating whatever it can catch.
D. stays with its pod until it is grown.

(G) **2.** When the killers hunted the smaller dolphins, they

A. were "each on their own."
B. kept circling until the dolphins tired.
C. hunted in a group.
D. ate their prey once they drew blood.

(G) **3.** People who study the "talking" of killer whales have found that

A. pods have rules for talking.
B. their one way of talking is to make a whistle through their blowholes.
C. killers are silent most of the time.
D. they love to "talk" so much they never wait for another pod member to finish.

Directions: Complete these sentences.

(SM) **4.** The author of this passage has an idea he wants to prove about killer whales. He states his idea, or THESIS, in Paragraph ____.

(SM) **5.** What killer whales really are (their species) is told in Paragraph ____.

(SM) **6.** Their family set-up is told about in Paragraph ____ .

(SM) **7.** The way the killers talk to each other is found in Paragraph ____ .

(G) **8.** The idea the author has about killer whales (his THESIS), which he proves all through the passage, is that killer whales are ________________

____ .

21

Rod Laver was a tennis "great." He was top man on the court for thirteen years, from 1962 to 1975. Whenever he got behind, the "Little Giant" didn't tighten up. Instead, he relaxed. He didn't start to play a "safe" game. He took chances. He played as if he was ahead. And more times than not it paid off.

We meet fear and worry every day. But when fear and worry cause us to lose our head, things get really bad. During the 1930's we were in deep trouble as a country. One out of three people was out of work. F.D.R. said, "The only thing we have to fear is fear itself." He knew that if Americans looked at their troubles with a clear head, they would work out of them.

Did you ever hear the story of Kelly? One day, Kelly walked over to his neighbor Casey to borrow his wheelbarrow. On the way Kelly started to think. "What if Casey isn't home?" A few steps further the thought hit Kelly, "What if his wheelbarrow is broken?" Kelly was getting more and more upset. "What if," Kelly began to say to himself, "What if Casey *won't* lend me the wheelbarrow?"

By the time he rang Casey's bell, Kelly was in an angry mood. Casey came to the door and greeted Kelly in a friendly way. Kelly pulled back and let Casey have one on the jaw. "Keep your darn wheelbarrow," growled Kelly as he walked back to his house.

PASSAGE 21 QUESTIONS

Directions: Circle the letter of the choice that best completes each thought below.

(D) **1.** When Rod Laver, the "Little Giant" of world tennis, got behind, he would

A. play a "safe" game.
B. play as if every point counted.
C. play a relaxed game.
D. forget what the score was.

(D) **2.** F.D.R.'s saying "the only thing we have to fear is fear itself" meant that

A. Americans would lose if they gave way to panic.
B. Americans had no real troubles during the 1930's.
C. F.D.R. would solve America's problems because *he* was not afraid.
D. Americans were in trouble because they hadn't looked at their troubles with clear heads.

(D) **3.** Kelly's main problem was that

A. he didn't have a wheelbarrow.
B. his neighbor, Casey, wouldn't lend him his wheelbarrow.
C. he let his worries take over until he believed them.
D. he was "sore" at Casey.

Directions: Complete these sentences.

(SM) **4.** A good title for this passage would be

____

(G) **5.** What Rod Laver and F.D.R. had in common was the ability to

____

(SIG) **6.** The advice of this passage is to

____

22

1. In 1928 Moe Berg led American League catchers in least number of errors. That season he got 101 base hits out of 107 games. He hit .287 and was up for the Most Valuable Player award.

2. But Moe Berg is not talked about only as a ball player. Moe was also an amazing scholar. He got a degree from Princeton. He spoke and wrote twelve languages. He knew Greek, Latin, and Sanskrit. And he read newspapers from all over the world.

Go on to next page. ➤

3. Moe was "nutty" about newspapers. They were piled all over the chairs, tables, and beds in his house. No one could move them. "They're alive," Moe would tell his roommate. "When they're dead, I'll let you move them." From his newspapers Moe learned about the world.

---

4. Moe got on "Information Please." Baseball leaders wanted Moe to go on the radio program. They felt it would help to show that ball players weren't dumb. Moe got ten thousand phone calls to N.B.C. after his first show!

---

5. H. G. Salinger of the *Detroit News* wanted to nail Moe. So he got a group of newsmen together to try to stump him. Moe agreed to go on one more program. Then he'd quit.

---

6. "Who or what are the Seven Sleepers, the Seven Wise Masters, the Seven Wise Men, the Seven Wonders of the World, and the Seven Stars?" the newsmen asked Moe.

"Professor" Berg took the first one. "The Seven Sleepers were seven youths of Ephesus, in Greece. King Decius put them in a cave. They slept, the story goes, for two hundred years."

"The Seven Wise Masters? That's the name of an Oriental book of tales. They tell of a son of a king. He was taught by seven wise masters. He studied the stars. He found out that he would die if he spoke within seven days. By not speaking, he lived."

"The Seven Wise Men? These were the Seven Sages of Greece, I think," said Moe. "They were Periander of Corinth, Pitacus of Mitylene, Thales of Miketus, Solon of Athens, Bias of Priene, Chilo of Sparta, and Cleobulus of Lindus."

"The Seven Wonders of the World were seven monuments. They were the pyramids of Egypt, the hanging gardens of Babylon, the Temple of Diana at Ephesus, the statue of Jupiter at Athens, the Tomb of Helicarnassus, the Colossus of Rhodes, and the Pharos, or lighthouse, of Alexandria."

"And the Seven Stars, Professor?" asked the newsmen.

"You are talking about the Pliades in the group of stars known as the Bull," said Moe.

---

7. The newsmen thought they could stump Moe by coming up to more modern times.

"Who was Calamity Jane?" they asked.

"Her real name," said the Professor, "was Jane Burke. She was an Indian scout like Buffalo Bill. She was an aide to General Custer and General Miles. Later she carried the mail between Deadwood, South Dakota and Custer, Montana."

The newsmen were knocked out of the box. Moe had "batted" 1000!

PASSAGE 22 QUESTIONS

Directions: Complete these sentences.

(SM) **1.** Section 1 talks about Moe's ________________ .

(SM) **2.** Section 2 talks about ________________ .

(SM) **3.** Section 3 talks about ________________ .

(SM) **4.** Section 4 talks about ________________ .

(SM) **5.** Section 5 talks about ________________ .

(SM) **6.** Section 6 is about Moe's ________________ .

Directions: Circle **True** or **False** for each sentence.

(G) **7.** Moe's claim to baseball fame was based solely on his hitting ability. True False

(G) **8.** Even though he didn't go to college, Moe was an amazing scholar. True False

(G) **9.** To make Moe—a famous ball player—look good on the air, the newsmen asked him an easy question. True False

(G) **10.** Moe was just as good with questions about modern times as he was with questions about ancient times. True False

Directions: Answer this question.

(C) **11.** This passage gives many people who read it a good deal of satisfaction. Why do you think this is so?

____

23

1. When we think about horses, we're apt to think about the sleek thoroughbreds at the track. Or else we picture people in riding habits walking horses along some woodland path. Yet, aside from racing or riding for pleasure, for thousands of years the horse has helped man get his daily work done.

2. In England, for example, horses worked alongside the Iron Horse—as the railroad was called. Horses helped build the railways. Horses carried workmen to their work stations. They shunted railway cars from track to track. This was a highly skilled action. The "shunter" horse had to work to a sharp word of command. He learned to take a grip on the track with his hind feet to start the great weight of the rail car. Cart horses were used. They wore a heavy harness with chain traces. Often horses were worked in pairs.

3. Another horse whose work was like the shunter was the "barge" horse. These were small cart horses. The barges along the canals were tied to the horses by long ropes from the bows of the barge. Barge horses walked along the tow paths of rivers and canals. They pulled as much as 50 tons. The barge horses became very expert at the start-off pull. The horses could take the weight at the right moment. Later when tractors were first used to pull the barges, a few were pulled into the canal by the backlash of the boats.

4. One tough job for horses was pulling bathing machines into the ocean at beaches. When bathing first became popular in England, ladies were too modest to be seen on a beach in their bathing suits. So they stepped into the "bathing machines" and were pulled by horses into the water. Bathing machines were wooden huts on wheels, with doors and steps leading from them. When the horses got the huts into deep enough water, the lady could get wet without being seen from the beach. This work was hard on the horses, but the sea water was good for their legs.

5. Horses were also used by undertakers. Only stallions were used. Neither mares nor geldings have the same gleaming jet-black coat as a stallion. The harness was black, with silver fittings. Long black loin cloths were draped on the horses' quarters, reaching almost to the ground. Matching ostrich feather plumes nodded on the horses' heads. Driven in pairs, or four-in-hand, they drew the hearses proudly.

6. Breweries used horses that were heavy, strong, and slow-moving. But these horses were easy to work with and smart. They learned to stand still while deliveries were made, to obey commands, and to take the weight of the huge beer wagons. And, often, after a hard day's work, they knew how to bring the tired and tipsy drivers home to the brewery.

PASSAGE 23 QUESTIONS

Directions: Match the item in Column **A** with the type of work in Column **B**. Write the correct letter on each line.

(D) **1.**

A	B
______ stallions	a. railroads
______ modest ladies	b. canal barges
______ small cart horses	c. beer wagons
______ the "shunter" horse	d. bathing machines
______ smart horses	e. undertakers' horses

Directions: Next to each subject write the number of the paragraph that deals with it.

(SM) **2.** a. Brewery horses ______

b. Railroad horses ______

c. Bathing machine horses ______

d. Canal barges ______

e. Undertakers' horses ______

Directions: Complete this sentence.

(G) **3.** The passage, as a whole, supports the idea that

____

____

24

1. A *zombie* is a part of the belief in voodoo magic. The word *zombie* comes from the Congo. It means one of the living dead. In voodoo, the living dead are corpses who have been revived by a sorcerer. Once he does this, the sorcerer has a slave. The zombie acts dazed—like a robot. It has no will, is stupid, and does not enjoy what it does. It speaks in a nasal tone.

2. Believers in voodoo will tell you that when a Haitian sorcerer needs a zombie, he first chooses his victim. Then he rides backwards to the victim's house after dark. He puts his mouth to a crack in the door. Then he sucks out the victim's soul. The victim dies. As soon as the body is buried, the sorcerer goes to the grave at midnight. He brings the soul in a bottle. After he digs up the body, he wakes the corpse by passing the soul under its nose. He also bangs it on the head. Then he leads the zombie away.

3. The zombie is used as a servant. It is overworked and whipped. It eats poor food. It must not be given salt because that would restore its will-power. Some sorcerers turn the zombie into stone. They keep it in front of the house. Others change it into an animal. They sell it as meat. One Haitian woman once dropped a piece of meat three times. Then she knew it came from a zombie.

4. Families try to save their kin from being turned into zombies. Some bury a body face down. They leave a dagger for protection. The body cannot be revived if it does not answer the call of the sorcerer. So the mouth is often sewn up.

5. So much for zombies as part of voodoo. In fact, many so-called zombies are simply slow-witted people. Being retarded, they look dazed and robot-like. There is a drug made from the root of an African tree that can cause a trance-like state. The use of this drug may have led to the belief in zombies.

PASSAGE 24 QUESTIONS

Directions: Circle the letter of the choice that best completes each thought below.

(D) **1.** In voodoo, the zombies
- A. are robots.
- B. are living dead.
- C. live in the Congo.
- D. are sorcerers.

(D) **2.** To obtain a zombie, the sorcerer should not
- A. capture the soul of his victim.
- B. ride backward to his victim's house before dark.
- C. bang his victim on the head.
- D. wait until his victim is buried.

(D) **3.** Families who want to protect their dead kin
- A. often stand guard at the grave.
- B. may sew up the mouth of the dead person.
- C. are helpless before the sorcerer's tricks.
- D. keep weapons away from the grave.

(D) **4.** "Zombies"
- A. are the helpless victims of voodoo.
- B. are always victims of an African drug.
- C. are found only in Africa.
- D. may be retarded people.

(SM) **5.** Paragraph 1 tells
- A. what zombies are.
- B. where zombies come from.
- C. what kind of people usually become zombies.
- D. about voodoo magic.

(SM) **6.** Paragraph 2 is mainly about
- A. believers in voodoo.
- B. the zombie's soul.
- C. how zombies die.
- D. how sorcerers get zombies.

(SM) **7.** The best title for Paragraph 3 would be "The
- A. Care of Zombies."
- B. Wages of Zombies."
- C. Eating of Zombies."
- D. Fate of Zombies."

(G) **8.** If we believe in voodoo magic, a zombie
- A. cannot feel suffering.
- B. has a fate worse than death.
- C. is a rare thing.
- D. should be shunned.

(C) **9.** A belief in voodoo would make a person's life more
- A. horrible.
- B. interesting.
- C. carefree.
- D. enjoyable.

25

1. The great stars of baseball come back to Yankee Stadium each year. In 1971 the lineup was: Phil Rizzuto, Bobby Brown, Don Larsen, Allie Reynolds, Yogi Berra, Billy Martin, Whitey Ford, and Micky Mantle. Each was cheered lustily. Then came the man "they save for last"—Joe DiMaggio. As Joe jogged to his place in line, the fans went wild. Here was the greatest of them all. In 1969 Joe had, in fact, been voted Greatest Living Player in a nationwide vote.

2. In his heyday, Joe DiMaggio was supreme. He was an all-around player. He was one of the two or three best batters in baseball history—up there with the Babe himself. He could hit the toughest pitchers. He even caught on to Bob Feller. He hit Feller often.

3. Joe's fielding was classic. He always knew where the ball was going. And Joe was there under it. He was by far the best base-runner in any league. He took off at the crack of his bat. He knew how much he could take. Time and again he stretched a single line-drive into a double or a triple.

4. He was a team leader. He powered the Yankees for many years. He studied the game. He knew the players. Joe gave advice: how to pitch, where to hit, where to stand in the outfield. His advice was heeded. Joe was so much a leader that when the men won extra money in the World Series, it was Joe they got to divide it up among them.

PASSAGE 25 QUESTIONS

Directions: Circle the letter of the choice that best completes the thought below.

(G) **1.** The reason Joe was supreme in his heyday was

A. he was a great batter.
B. he was an all-around player.
C. his fielding was classic.
D. he was a team leader.

Directions: Answer these questions.

(G) **2.** In 1971, when the stars of baseball lined up in Yankee Stadium, why did Joe DiMaggio take his place last?

____

____

(D) **3.** What do you think the writer means when he says Joe's fielding was "classic"?

____

____

____

Directions: Choose a title for each paragraph. Write the title after the paragraph number.

(SM) **4.**

Paragraph	**Titles**
1. ____________________	"The Greatest"
2. ____________________	"Joe's Fielding and Base-Running"
3. ____________________	"Team Leader"
4. ____________________	"Good Batter"

26

The fans had a special feeling about Joe DiMaggio. He was not only a great athlete. He was a man.

True, he had a big ego. But he wasn't sick with ego the way many stars get. He looked at himself as a member of the Yankee team.

Joe did have confidence in himself. He knew he could hit. He would stand up at the plate, lift his bat, and wait for the pitch. When it came, he watched it break, and then, wham! He never flinched from a close ball.

One season he was hitting around .470. He asked his pal Lefty Gomez, "Anybody hit .500 in this league?" Gomez thought Joe was crazy.

But Joe put the team first, himself second. During his last few years with the Yankees his injuries caught up with him. His heel hurt badly. His back gave him trouble. He couldn't pull the ball around to left field in his last year. But Joe never moaned about his pain. He played hard. He kept pushing to steal bases. The Yankees needed them. He had spikes built up on his shoes to take the pressure off his heel. It was agony for him to get in and out of a cab. But on the field Joe gave all he had. The fans came to see a ball game. Joe gave it to them.

Joe had his image to live up to. Take a little thing. Joe liked to read *Superman Comics*. He'd walk his friend Lefty Gomez up to a newsstand. "Lefty, what day is today?"

Lefty would play dumb. "Today is Wednesday."

"No, it's not Wednesday, it's the day the new Superman comes out." Then he'd get Lefty to buy the copy. It just wouldn't look right for Joe DiMaggio to be seen buying a comic book.

PASSAGE 26 QUESTIONS

Directions: Answer these questions. Write your answer on the lines after the question.

(G) **1.** How do you know that Joe DiMaggio wasn't "sick with ego"?

____

____

(G) **2.** What do the words, "The fans came to see a ball game. Joe gave it to them," tell you about Joe DiMaggio as a man?

____

____

(G) **3.** Joe got Lefty Gomez to buy his comic book. What does that tell you about Joe as a person?

____

____

(SM) **4.** The first part of the Joe DiMaggio story told you about him as a player. With what side of Joe does this second part deal?

____

____

27

If you sum up Joe DiMaggio, it's a matter of style. Joe just didn't make a fuss. He let his deeds speak for him. He'd help many a rookie fielder find the right place to field the next hit. Joe would just make a little motion to guide his teammate. The fans didn't see it. No big deal.

You see Joe's style clearly in the way he ended his famous hitting streak. It was the 1941 season. The record for hits in straight games had stood since 1897. Wee Willie Keeler of Baltimore had hit in 44 games. As the summer wore on, Joe's streak went from the sports page to the front page. His teammates were nervous wrecks. When would it end? Pressure mounted. Each game there was only one thought in the minds of the fans: Would DiMag hit?

July 17, 1941 was a night game. Joe had hit in 55 straight games. Joe slammed an inside ball to third base. Ken Keltner backhanded the ball and threw Joe out at first. The same thing happened in the seventh. In the eighth Joe drove a line grounder toward center field. Lou Boudreau, the shortstop, caught it. An underhand throw to Ray Mack on second and a throw to first by Mack made it a double play. Joe was out. That was Joe's last chance in that game.

The stretch was history. Joe trotted up the dugout ramp, and walked into the clubhouse. The locker room was quiet. Would Joe be bitter? The Yankees had won. But everything had gone against Joe in the game.

"Well," said Joe, loudly enough for all his teammates to hear, "that's over." It was all he said.

PASSAGE 27 QUESTIONS

Directions: Answer these questions. Write your answer on the lines after the question.

(G) **1.** How did Joe take the ending of his hitting streak?

(G) **2.** Why did Joe make "a little motion" when he helped a rookie find a hit?

(G) **3.** What kind of person was Joe DiMaggio, as far as this passage goes?

(SM) **4.** What does it mean to say that, "if you sum Joe DiMaggio up, it's a matter of style"?

28

We can make mistakes at any age. Some mistakes we make are about money. But most mistakes are about people. "Did Jerry *really* care when I broke up with Helen?" "When I got that great job, did Jim really feel good about it, as a friend? Or did he envy my luck?" "And Paul—why didn't I pick up that he was friendly just because I had a car?" When we look back, doubts like these can make us feel bad. But when we look back, it's too late.

Why do we go wrong about our friends—or our enemies? Sometimes what people say hides their real meaning. And if we don't really listen, we miss the feeling behind the words. Suppose someone tells you, "You're a lucky dog." Is he really on your side? If he says, "You're a lucky guy" or "You're a lucky gal," that's being friendly. But "lucky dog"? There's a bit of envy in those words. Maybe he doesn't see it himself. But bringing in the "dog" bit puts you down a little. What he may be saying is that he doesn't think you deserve your luck.

"Just think of all the things you have to be thankful for" is another noise that says one thing and means another. It could mean that the speaker is trying to get you to see your problem as part of your life as a whole. But is he? Wrapped up in this phrase is the thought that your problem isn't important. It's telling you to think of all the starving people in the world when you haven't got a date for Saturday night.

How can you tell the real meaning behind someone's words? One way is to take a good look at the person talking. Do his words fit the way he looks? Does what he says square with the tone of voice? His posture? The look in his eyes? Stop and think. The minute you spend thinking about the *real* meaning of what people say to you may save another mistake.

PASSAGE 28 QUESTIONS

Directions: Circle the letter of the choice that best completes each thought below.

(D) **1.** In the first paragraph, the writer recalls some things that happened between him and his friends. He

A. feels happy, thinking of how nice his friends were to him.

B. feels he may not have "read" his friends' true feelings correctly.

C. thinks it was a mistake to have broken up with his girl friend, Helen.

D. is sorry that his friends let him down.

(D) **2.** In the second paragraph, the writer talks about someone saying, "You're a lucky dog." He is saying that

A. the speaker of this sentence is just being friendly.

B. this saying means the same as "You're a lucky guy" or "You're a lucky gal."

C. the word "dog" shouldn't be used to apply to people.

D. sometimes the words used by a speaker give a clue to the feeling behind the words.

(SM) **3.** This passage tries to tell you how to

A. avoid mistakes about money and friends.

B. "size up" people.

C. avoid mistakes in understanding what people tell you.

D. keep people friendly without trusting them.

(G) **4.** In listening to a person the important thing is

A. to notice his tone, his posture, and the look in his eye.

B. to listen to how he pronounces his words.

C. to check his words against his manner, his tone of voice, and his posture.

D. not to believe what he says.

Directions: Complete this sentence.

(SIG) **5.** If you followed the advice of the writer, you would

____

____

____

29

Joan of Arc, as you know, died trying to drive the English from her country. She gave up the safety of her life as a farm girl to follow an ideal. In modern times John Brown also followed an ideal when he led his raid on Harper's Ferry.

John Brown believed in God. When he was young, he had taken a young runaway slave into his home. He hated slavery and felt it was against God's will. During the battle over Kansas, Brown and his sons had fought hard against the men who wanted Kansas to be a slave state.

In 1859, he came East to strike a strong blow against slavery. With him, in a farmhouse outside the town of Harper's Ferry, Virginia, were twenty-one followers, five of them black men. Brown had picked Harper's Ferry, which lay between the Shenandoah and the Potomac Rivers, with care. It was on the border of Pennsylvania, a free state. Brown felt that the slaves he would free would easily get across the border to "free" land. Behind Harper's Ferry lay hilly country, where Brown and his men could hide out if the raid failed.

As Brown and his men made their way into Harper's Ferry on the night of October 16, 1859, Brown told his men, "Word will soon spread throughout the countryside. Slaves will take up hatchets, guns, and knives. They will join us."

But Brown's raid fizzled. His men did take over the Rifle House and the Engine House (locomotives from the railroad that went through town were sometimes kept there). And Brown took a number of hostages as the fighting spread. But word of the raid reached the Charles Town militia. The next day Brown was holed up in the Engine House with the hostages. The militia kept firing. When Brown sent a man with an offer of truce, he was shot down. The townspeople and the militia were out for Brown's blood.

The next day Colonel Robert E. Lee and a group of U.S. Marines drew up before the Engine House. The hostages had gone without food for two days. They were afraid for their lives. During the entire time of the raid, no slaves had joined Brown.

Lee sent word to Brown to surrender. Brown asked to be allowed to escape with his men. Lee refused. He sent in twelve marines. Five minutes later it was all over. Most of Brown's men were dead. Two marines were killed. Brown lay on the grass in front of the Engine House bleeding from sword wounds. He was taken to the jail. He was charged with treason and murder. Thirty-seven days later he was hung.

PASSAGE 29 QUESTIONS

Directions: Circle the letter of the choice that best completes each thought below.

(D) **1.** The author compares John Brown to Joan of Arc because both

A. were killed.
B. believed in God.
C. followed an ideal.
D. were unmarried.

(D) **2.** The article tells that Kansas

A. became a free state.
B. was part of the "underground railroad."
C. was where Brown grew up.
D. was where Brown had fought slavery.

(D) **3.** Harper's Ferry

A. was carefully chosen by Brown.
B. never had a railroad.
C. was in flat country.
D. was in "free" land.

(G) **4.** John Brown's real fight—as he saw it—was with

A. the Charles Town Militia.
B. U.S. society as a whole.
C. Robert E. Lee.
D. the slaveholders.

Directions: Answer these questions.

(SM) **5.** What do the third and fourth paragraphs deal with?

____

(C) **6.** Do you think that John Brown was a failure? ______________

Tell why or why not. ______________________________

____

____

____

30

Johnny Miller is tall and slim. He has a head of blond hair. He has good looks. His golf swing is also beautiful. He can drive a ball very, very far. But it is his concentration that has made him a star. In 1974 he won three straight tournaments. Nobody ever did that.

"Every time I draw the club back," says Miller, "I know I'm going to hit solid. The putts seem to fly off the putter and go right into the middle of the hole. It makes the game look easy."

Miller started as a teenager. He came up fast. "When I finished second in the Masters, I knew," he recalls, "that I could play with the big boys."

He thinks a golfer's game is in his head. He writes little rules for himself on a piece of brown envelope. "Take the club back slowly." "You must keep your head still." "Make sure you are comfortable before starting the swing." He admits this sounds "corny," but he feels each saying has a purpose. "I believe the brain is a computer," says Miller. "If you feed things into the brain, it sends them to the body. All my sayings are positive. They are commands."

Miller seems aloof on the golf course. "I must concentrate. I must think out each shot. That way I keep from falling into bad habits." If his concentration does not fail him, Miller is sure he will go on to become an all-time golfing great.

PASSAGE 30 QUESTIONS

Directions: Circle the letters of the choices that best complete each thought below.

(D) **1.** Three facts the writer gives to show that Miller is good are:

A. he drives far.
B. he finished second in the Masters.
C. he is blond, tall, and slim.
D. he putts well.

(D) **2.** Miller bases his game on

A. using his brain as a computer.
B. his beautiful swing.
C. "corny" rules.
D. staying aloof on the golf course.

(D) **3.** Miller thinks the most important thing in golf is

A. your build.
B. your head.
C. your manner on the course.
D. to make the game took easy.

Directions: Write the answers to these questions.

(SM) **4.** What would be a good title for this passage?

____

(G) **5.** According to the author, what kind of golfer is Johnny Miller?

____

31

1. Jockeys are the smallest athletes. They are rarely over five feet six, or 120 pounds. The lighter the weight on the horse, the faster it can go.

---

2. Riding fast horses on the track is tough on the small jockeys. The jockey doesn't "sit" on the horse. He leans forward on his legs. The strain is on his thighs and calf muscles. As jockeys age, their legs "go" first. Jockeys also need arm strength. It's a strain holding a 1,000-pound racehorse.

On muddy days, jockeys get a pounding of mud. The mud comes flying off the hooves of the horses in front. "It feels like someone is punching you all over," says one rider.

And a jockey can be hurt. A jockey can have a leg jammed between two horses. Or it can get caught between his horse and the rail. The worst accidents are from falls. A horse may fall on his rider. Or horses behind may trample him if he hits the track. In one year about 240 riders are hurt badly. That's one out of six jockeys.

---

3. But the jockeys are well paid. A jockey keeps about ten percent of the money his horses win. Jacinto Vasquez, a five-foot-three comer, has ridden horses to $7,000,000 in wins in the last eight years. Which means he does almost $100,000 a year.

---

4. Why do some jockeys do better than others? "It isn't the way a boy sits on a horse or uses the reins or the whip," says Conn McCreary. McCreary was a top jockey of the 1950's. He rode two Kentucky Derby winners. "Most jockeys do this the same. It's the 'feel' he has for the horses."

"When you come right down to it, it just seems that horses run better for some riders," McCreary says. "A real good jockey doesn't lose with the best horse. And sometimes he'll win with the second or third best."

Many Latin-American riders, like Jacinto, seem to have the knack. "Maybe it's because we grew up with horses," says Jacinto. "Maybe it's because we like to ride. There was a strike at Aqueduct last year. Me, Jorge Velasquez, and Angel Cordero (two other top Latin riders) went to a park. We rented horses, and rode around the bridle path!"

PASSAGE 31 QUESTIONS

Directions: If the sentence is true, circle **True**. If the sentence is false, circle **False**.

(D) **1.** There is no good reason—except custom—that jockeys are small. True False

(D) **2.** The worst accident that can happen to a jockey is to catch his leg between his horse and the rail. True False

(D) **3.** Win or lose, you get high pay as a jockey. True False

(D) **4.** Jacinto Vasquez and his friends rode horses on their day off when there was a strike at Aqueduct. True False

Directions: This article deals with some of the sides of a jockey's life. For each section, fill in the main subject that the paragraphs in the section deal with:

(SM) **5.** Section 1 deals with ____________________

____

Section 2 deals with ____________________

____

Section 3 deals with ____________________

____

Section 4 deals with ____________________

____

Directions: Complete this sentence.

(G) **6.** A good jockey is a jockey who ____________________

____

____

32

A rattlesnake's strike is an example of very advanced natural development. The snake attacks from an S position. In the strike, the snake moves out about a third to a half of its length. It's like the short jab of a boxer, and has about the same impact. The snake can lash straight out, or it can, if necessary, strike straight up.

High speed photography shows that the mouth is open at the start of the strike. As the snake moves, its fangs, which lie along the roof of the mouth and are retractable, snap into position. At the moment of impact the mouth is wide open and the fangs are fully extended. The fangs are like long hypodermic needles. They are hollow from the venom sac to the tip. The strike is swift; the fangs go in, the poison is punched into the wound, the snake retracts its fangs, and moves back into its S position, ready to strike again. All of this happens in the time it takes a man to blink his eyelid.

Unlike the rattler, with its long, retractable fangs, the cobra's fangs are fixed. Because they are fixed, they must be shorter. The cobra must get closer to its victim, and stay longer while it embeds its venom. Thus the cobra is open to counterattack while it is biting. On the other hand, there is little chance that the rattler's victim will strike back, dazed as it is from the force and swiftness of the rattler's strike.

PASSAGE 32 QUESTIONS

Directions: If the sentence is true, circle **True.** If the sentence is false, circle **False**.

(D) **1.** The rattler always strikes straight out, from an S position. True False

(D) **2.** Although the rattler's strike is poisonous, it has little force. In fact, it happens so fast, the animal bitten may not even be sure it was bitten. True False

(D) **3.** A rattler's fangs lie along the roof of its mouth when not in action. True False

(D) **4.** As soon as the fangs enters a victim, the poison flows through the fangs and into the wound, with no effort on the snake's part. True False

(D) **5.** The cobra, being deadlier than the rattlesnake, is a more able attacker than the rattler. True False

(D) **6.** The rattler strikes swiftly. True False

(D) **7.** The rattler's fangs are fixed at the front of the mouth. True False

(D) **8.** The rattler is a more able attacker than a cobra. True False

(D) **9.** The rattler's fangs are short, so that its poison does not have far to flow. True False

Directions: Complete these sentences.

(SM) **10.** A good title to tell what this passage is about would be ____________

____

(G) **11.** The many details in the passage about the rattler show that its strike

____

(G) **12.** The sentence that is backed up by the rest of the passage is:

____

____

33

Tatanka Iyotake, Sitting Bull, grew up along the Grand River in Dakota country. In his teens he learned to hunt buffalo. And the braves let him come along on a raid for horses against the Crow.

Now, he was thirty, and a chief. It was the summer of 1864. His people, the Hunkpapas, were camped along the Little Missouri in the Teton Mountain range. They had seen other tribes go onto the reservations. But they were still free. George Catlin, the painter, had visited the Hunkpapa camp in 1832. But he could not get them to pose for him. He wrote: "The Hunkpapas are those who camp alone."

Along the Little Missouri the hunting was good. Every *tipi* had meat drying for the cold months to come. The ponies grew sleek from the good prairie grass. There was time to lie in the sun. Play with the children. Study the blue sky. And listen to bird songs. Sitting Bull had a feeling for birds—eagles, magpies, and meadowlarks. He felt he could talk with meadowlarks. He felt they would tell him if danger was near.

Sitting Bull had seen the fate of other tribes. He went to see his woodland cousins on the reservations. Their land had been taken. They had been driven from their homes. Proud hunters had to learn to dig in the earth with hoes. The game was scarce. The water was not fit to drink. So, to any white men who came asking for land, Sitting Bull said, "Leave us alone. We want only to be left alone."

PASSAGE 33 QUESTIONS

Directions: Complete these statements.

(G) **1.** The writer tells you that George Catlin, the painter, could not get the Hunkpapas to pose for him to show you that

____

(G) **2.** The writer tells you about the life of Sitting Bull's people along the Little Missouri to show you that

____

(G) **3.** The writer tells you about what happened to Indians on the reservations to show you

____

Directions: Answer this question. Write your answer on the lines after the question.

(SM) **4.** In this first part of the Sitting Bull story, what is the conflict the writer has told you of?

____

____

____

34

But the white men were on the move. Up the Missouri they came. They cut the trees to fuel the steamboats. They killed all the beaver. The miners wanted gold. The trappers wanted fur. The government men wanted power. And the army men wanted glory. The Indian was in the way.

That autumn some Santees came to Sitting Bull's camp. They said that General Alfred Sully was near. He was bringing hundreds of soldiers from the Missouri River forts. These soldiers killed Indians wherever they found them. And put their heads on poles.

The Teton chiefs around Sitting Bull knew they were doomed. Run, or fight? Before they could decide, the soldiers found them at Kildeer Mountain.

This was the first time that Sitting Bull fought the blue-coats. Their skirmish lines were a mile long. Their rifles chattered. Cannon shot hurtled into the midst of the women and children trying to flee. The Indians' old muskets and arrows were no match for the blue-coats' rifles. But the Indians fought like surrounded buffaloes. They were able to scatter to the hills.

Sitting Bull went further north and west. He camped west of the Black Hills. Here in unspoiled country fed by clear streams—the Powder, the Rosebud, and Big Horn—he knew he must not give up more land. He sent his braves against Army wagon trains that came up over the Bozeman Trail. He fought with General Connor's men. These soldiers had standing orders. The orders read: "Kill every male Indian over 12 years of age in the Powder River Country." These fights ended in the victory of Red Cloud's warriors at Fort Phil Kearny. Red Cloud was one of Sitting Bull's chiefs.

After the Battle of the Hundred Slain, the whites asked for peace. The U. S. Government Indian Office at Fort Peck in Montana asked Sitting Bull to come there to talk. Sitting Bull's answer was to send his brother-in-law Grey Eagle. "Go there," Sitting Bull told Techanke (Grey Eagle). "When you find a white man who tells the truth, return. Then I will go see him." Grey Eagle did not ask Sitting Bull to go to the Fort.

PASSAGE 34 QUESTIONS

Directions: Answer these questions. Write your answers on the lines.

(G) **1.** Why did the white man feel that the Indian was "in the way"?

____

____

(G) **2.** What was the result when Sitting Bull met the blue-coats for the first time?

____

____

(G) **3.** When Sitting Bull camped west of the Black Hills, what was the result of General Connor's move into the Powder River Country?

____

____

(G) **4.** Why didn't Sitting Bull go to Fort Peck?

____

____

Directions: Circle the letter of your choice.

(SM) **5.** Pick out the title that best tells what this passage is about.

A. The Rape of the Land
B. Defeat and Victory
C. Sitting Bull Retreats
D. The Whites Ask for Peace

35

On June 25, 1876, Lieutenant-Colonel George Custer led the Seventh Cavalry against Sitting Bull. Sitting Bull's tribe was camped along the Little Big Horn River. Why did Custer come to the Little Big Horn? The U.S. had a treaty with the Indians. This treaty gave the Indians the sacred *PAHA SAPA*—the Black Hills. But Custer, and General Phil Sheridan, felt there was gold in the Black Hills. Gold—and glory. With his Seventh Cavalry Custer took a newsman, Mark Kellogg. He also took two geologists. And newspapers ran headlines: RICH MINES OF GOLD AND SILVER FOUND BY CUSTER.

Before Custer's march, Sitting Bull had told his people of his Sun Dance vision. "I looked into the sky and saw soldiers on horses. They came down like grasshoppers. Their heads were down. Their hats fell off. They fell right into our camp. . ." As we know, Custer and his men were killed to the last man.

After the battle, Sitting Bull talked with Father Jean Genin when he stayed with the Hunkpapas. "It did not last long enough to light a pipe. We were camped awaiting the will of the Great Spirit. When the soldiers came, my men killed the last of them in a short time. Yet what did I do? The Great Spirit saved our lives. They should accuse the Great Spirit. He saved us by letting them die. We did not go out of our country to kill them. They came to kill us and got killed themselves."

PASSAGE 35 QUESTIONS

Directions: Answer these questions. Write your answers on the lines.

(G) **1.** Why did Custer go to the Little Big Horn?

____

(G) **2.** What did it mean when, in Sitting Bull's vision, he saw "their heads were down; their hats fell off"?

____

____

(G) **3.** How did Sitting Bull feel about killing Custer's men?

(SM) **4.** What does this part of the Sitting Bull story deal mainly with?

(C) **5.** What kind of person would you say Sitting Bull was?

36

1. After Custer's death, the hunt was on. There was no
hiding place. The farther north Sitting Bull went, the closer
came the white men. Sitting Bull took his people to Canada—
2. Grandmother's country. The Canadians gave them no help.
They wanted them off their hands. With too little land to hunt,
the Indians were cold and hungry. They did not have skins to
build tipis. The cloth tipis they had were cold in winter, hot in
summer. Sitting Bull went back across the U. S. border. He
3. looked old and beaten. Yet, when he gave his rifle to the
soldier chief at Fort Buford, his voice was firm. "I wish to be
remembered," he said, "as the last Indian to give up my rifle."

PASSAGE 36 QUESTIONS

Directions: Complete these statements.

(G) **1.** While in Canada, the Indians' basic lack was

(G) **2.** To the very last, Sitting Bull showed that

(SM) **3.** This passage can be looked at as having three sections. Section 1 tells about Sitting Bull's retreat; Section 2 tells of his Canadian stay; and Section 3 tells of his

37

The line "Me Tarzan—you Jane" is always good for a laugh. But for every gagman who gets laughs at Tarzan's expense there are a hundred people in all walks of life who have become his loyal fans.

The Tarzan cult is made up mainly of men who read Edgar Rice Burroughs' Tarzan books in the 1930's. "But younger people are getting into it in growing numbers," says Vernell Coriell, founder of the E.R.B. (Edgar Rice Burroughs) Club. "Many teenagers were at the dumdum we held last year at the sci-fi meeting in Toronto." A "dumdum," Coriell told me, was a ritual feast held by apes. Tarzan, you may recall, was the only human who could get into a dumdum.

Tarzan fans have gone to great lengths to show how they feel about the master of the jungle. Bill Dutcher, a cook in Sacramento, sometimes swings from trees. A student in Utah made a movie about Tarzan. For Tarzan's victory yell he found that an off-key violin, the howl of a hyena, and the growl of a dog did the trick. And other fans have saved Tarzan bubble gum, Tarzan T-shirts, and, of course, Tarzan books.

Why a Tarzan cult? "I guess there were things about Tarzan that got to us when we read about him as kids," mused Dutcher at a Sacramento meeting of an E.R.B. Club. "Take the way Tarzan woke from sleep. If he had been sleeping in the jungle, he didn't get up punchy and dopey the way we get out of bed. He sat up instantly alert. Tarzan had a keen sense of smell—as keen as an animal. He could travel miles, swiftly, by swinging through the trees."

"You can get with Tarzan. He is the free man. He doesn't have to put up with bosses. Tarzan makes you feel big, and great."

PASSAGE 37 QUESTIONS

Directions: If the sentence is true, circle **True.** If the sentence is false, circle **False.**

(D) **1.** Most Tarzan fans are men past 50 years old. True False

(D) **2.** Teenage Tarzan fans were all at the dumdum in Toronto. True False

Directions: Which choice best completes each thought? Circle the letter.

(D) **3.** A cook in Sacramento swings from trees because

A. he likes the exercise.
B. he was in a Tarzan movie.
C. he admires Tarzan.
D. he likes to practice Tarzan's victory yell.

(SM) **4.** Two subjects this passage talks about are (Circle two letters.)

A. why some men like Tarzan.
B. why the line, "Me Tarzan, you Jane," is good for a laugh.
C. the facts about the Tarzan cult.
D. why Tarzan was better than people who get out of bed in bad shape.

(G) **5.** The main thing this passage proves is that

A. Tarzan should be admired by all.
B. Tarzan is just the interesting hero of Edgar Rice Burroughs's Tarzan books.
C. Tarzan lives.
D. old Tarzan books could be worth a lot of money.

(C) **6.** This passage could well lead us to believe that

A. people who believe in Tarzan have no reason why they do; they just like something from the past.
B. lots of Tarzan stuff — books, T-shirts, and so on — could be worth more as time goes on.
C. people who follow the Tarzan cult are not serious about it; they just do it for a gag — something to have fun with.
D. books have little to do with how people act in real life.

38

---

1. It was August 1942. The Panzers of the Afrika Korps under General Erwin Rommel had swept across the northern coast of Africa. Now the "Desert Fox" was set to take Cairo and Alexandria. Then he would try to seize the Suez Canal.

Facing Rommel was the British Eighth Army under General Montgomery. Monty's men were drawn up in front of the key town of El Alamein. Rommel's plan was to make a strong surprise attack across the Qattara lowlands. This was at the southern end of the British line. He would then sweep north with his panzers. He would roll the British into the sea.

Go on to next page. ➤

But Monty knew Rommel's plan. So he placed his guns in depth just where the "Desert Fox" would strike. Rommel moved on the day Monty expected. Even though the British were ready, it was a tough battle. Rommel's tanks fought hard. But Monty had had time to prepare. Rommel lost hundreds of tanks. Some ran out of fuel. Others were knocked out by the British guns. Monty followed up his victory. He chased the Afrika Korps from North Africa.

---

2. This story was repeated all through World War II. Time and again the German armies were met and defeated. The Americans and the British were always ready for them. It happened with Rommel in Africa, with Kluge in France, and with Runstedt in Germany. At one point in the war, when Rommel asked the German HQ to *repeat* a message, the Americans had the message *before* the Germans!

---

3. The secret of how the British broke the Germans' secret code is told in a book called *The Ultra Secret*. As far back as 1938, a Polish mechanic had been working in a factory in Eastern Germany. He judged that the machine he was working on was some sort of machine for sending coded messages. As a Pole, he didn't like the Germans very much. So he carefully noted the details of the parts. A year later he was smuggled out of Germany. He was set up in Paris by the French Secret Service. There he made a wooden mock-up of the code machine.

Later, the British Secret Service went this feat one better. They sent men to Poland. They succeeded, with the help of the Polish Underground, in getting a brand new Enigma machine, as it was called.

---

4. What did the machine do? It took a typed message and scrambled it. Then the scrambled message was sent by radio. Another machine received the signal and unscrambled the message. Hitler's Nazis thought they had the perfect code machine. They felt so secure that they used Enigma machines during all of World War II.

---

5. The British never tipped their hand. In 1940, Prime Minister Winston Churchill was called by the Secret Service.

The city of Coventry was to be bombed. The Service had intercepted a top-secret signal on the Enigma machine. The British could not let the Germans know they were getting Enigma signals. So Churchill decided not to give the people of Coventry warning to get out of the city. In the light of the use the Allies made of Enigma signals all through the war, Churchill made the right decision.

PASSAGE 38 QUESTIONS

Directions: Which choice best completes each thought? Circle the letter.

(D) **1.** Monty probably placed his guns
- A. near the sea.
- B. north of El Alamein.
- C. at the southern end of his men's lines.
- D. in none of the above places.

(G) **2.** The Americans and British often won because
- A. they were well supplied with guns and men.
- B. they knew the Nazi plans.
- C. their generals were smarter.
- D. the German tanks ran out of fuel.

(G) **3.** The British broke the Germans' secret code by
- A. getting an Enigma machine.
- B. typing the German messages and then unscrambling them.
- C. never "tipping their hand."
- D. knowing that any message sent by the Enigma machine had to be top secret.

Directions: Complete these statements.

(G) **4.** Prime Minister Churchill didn't warn the people of Coventry because

____

(SM) **5.** This passage has five sections. Each section tells one part of the Ultra Secret story.

A. Section 1 shows an example of how ______________________________

B. In Section 2, the author says that the way it went at El Alamein was the way it went all through the war. Section 2 is a comment on Section 1.

C. In Section 3 the author tells about how ______________________________

D. In Section 4 the writer tells how ______________________________

E. Section 5 shows how ______________________________

39

1. What's the sweetest candy you can eat? Sweeter than sugar? Sweeter than molasses? It's licorice in its pure form. The extract of the licorice root is fifty times sweeter than sugar. It's still "there" in water when it's only one part in 20,000.

---

2. Licorice is strange stuff. It's used in medicine—in cough syrups and throat lozenges. The tobacco industry uses lots of licorice. Licorice lends mildness to pipe tobacco, cigars, and cigarettes. It even helps keep tobacco fresh and moist.

---

3. Licorice comes from a plant. The licorice plant is two to five feet high. But it sends out underground runners sometimes 25 feet long. Licorice itself comes from the roots of the plant.

---

4. Licorice's real name is *glycyrrhiza.* It comes from two Greek words—*glykys* (sweet) and *rhiza* (root)—sweet root. The Greeks made up the name—so they must have known about it. In fact, Alexander the Great's soldiers carried licorice in their packs to ward off thirst. Archaeologists found it in the tomb of the Egyptian king Tutankhamen, who lived over 3,000 years ago. Even today, the Egyptians drink *maisus*—a sweet drink of licorice and water.

Licorice has indeed had a long history. In ancient China, licorice was used on Buddha's birthday. An extract of the licorice root was poured three times over Buddha's statue. Then the faithful were given spoonfuls of it. Today it's making a comeback. You don't have to wait for Buddha's birthday to get some licorice. You can go out and buy it at the nearest candy counter.

PASSAGE 39 QUESTIONS

Directions: If the sentence is true, circle **True**. If the sentence is false, circle **False**.

(D) **1.** Licorice tastes sweeter than sugar when it is only one part in 20,000 parts of water. True False

(D) **2.** When added to tobacco, licorice makes the tobacco milder. True False

(D) **3.** Licorice is taken from long underground runners of the glycyrrhiza plant. True False

(D) **4.** Licorice was known to the Greeks, Egyptians, and Chinese of olden times, but then forgotten until our day. True False

Directions: Think of good titles for the sections.

(SM) **5.** This passage has four sections. For each section, write a title showing what phase of the licorice story the writer talks about.

Section 1: ______________________________

Section 2: ______________________________

Section 3: ______________________________

Section 4: ______________________________

Directions: Which choice best completes each thought? Circle the letter.

(SM) **6.** One thing about licorice *not* talked about in this passage is

A. where it grows.
B. its use in medicine.
C. how to get it.
D. where it was known.

(G) **7.** Licorice

A. is popular today because it's a natural food.
B. while interesting, has been of little use to man.
C. used to be important years ago, but is just a little-known candy today.
D. has been of value to man.

40

"You don't listen!" says your girl friend.

When you answer, "But I do. I can repeat every word you just said!" it doesn't seem to be good enough.

"No," she says, "you don't listen."

What's wrong? Scientists tell us that words give us only 35 percent of what we mean. The rest? Body language. In other words, you may hear the words but not get the "tune."

Body language. You know about the hitchhiker's thumb. That sign is clear. But what's the sign for a pretty girl? An Arab strokes his beard. An Italian pulls on one of his ear lobes. An Englishman looks slowly away.

Body language, if you look for it, is all over the place. When two people like each other, they show it. Boys—and girls—hold their bodies straighter. Muscle-tone is higher. Sagging skin and pouches under their eyes may go away. Eyes are bright. Skin may be pinker. And each preens. The girl works with her hair. The boy combs his hair, straightens his tie—or his shirt—and pulls up his socks.

If the couple is going with each other, they look at each other a lot. They tilt their heads. A girl may cross her legs, place a hand on her hip, or lift her chest. And she may show her palm. Most of the time girls never show their palms. But when she's interested in a man, she shows her palm all over the place. She may even cover a cough from a cigarette by holding her palm out. The boy and girl are telling each other, and the world, that they are "that way" about each other.

Words are only part of talking. The rest takes in body movements, dress, and, of course, the tone of the voice. Recently I went to a meeting of some teachers. Two teachers were arguing. What the lady was *saying* was polite enough. Her voice, though, gave her away. It kept getting higher and more angry by the minute. She was *saying*—in words—that there were two sides to the matter. But what she was *really* saying—with her tone of voice—was "I hate you!" When the man told her that she was showing anger by her voice—and her whole body—she did not agree. She was not aware of her real feelings. But her body language told the story.

PASSAGE 40 QUESTIONS

Directions: Circle the letter of the choice that best completes each thought below.

(G) **1.** If you "hear the words, but don't get the tune," it means that you

A. didn't hear what the person said to you.
B. didn't get the person's real message.
C. didn't listen.
D. can't repeat every word he said.

(G) **2.** The passage does not tell you that a boy and a girl who like each show it by

A. talking.
B. posture.
C. looks.
D. sharpening up hair or clothes.

Directions: Write the answers.

(G) **3.** Name four things people use—whether they know it or not—to get their "message" across.

A. ______________________________

B. ______________________________

C. ______________________________

D. ______________________________

(SM) **4.** The writer tells about some situations that have to do with body language. How many of these situations does he talk about? __________

41

"Addicts will come to us and say, 'I'm sick and tired of this. I'm tired of committing crimes and running from the cops. I'm tired of feeding my habit. I want to make something of my life.' This type of person has the best chance to kick the habit." says George Carr, a forty-year-old former addict. Mr. Carr guides the York Street Clinic of Patrick House. Patrick House is a center for drug addicts in Jersey City.

Why is Patrick House successful? "For one thing," says Mr. Carr, "it has a group of 80 devoted workers. These workers relate to the ten or so patients they work with. They 'take an interest' in their patients' efforts to get better. For another, the program at Patrick House doesn't only treat the addict's habit. It offers aid for health, educational, and legal problems. Patrick House also has a dental clinic that Fairleigh Dickinson University operates for it. It helps the addict learn job skills."

Most important, Patrick House offers a methadone program. Methadone is an unusual drug. It substitutes for the addicts' need for heroin. But it does not produce the "high" that heroin does.

How does the methadone program work? "First," Mr. Carr explained, "there is the 'buildup.' Daily doses are increased. The addict develops a tolerance for methadone. He drinks the drug (in fruit juice) each day. A nurse is present. If he comes to the clinic in a 'high,' or drunk, he gets no methadone. His urine is checked three times a week for heroin and for other narcotics (barbiturates, cocaine, or amphetamines).

"After a few weeks, the patient no longer craves heroin. If he takes heroin while he has methadone in him, he doesn't get the 'high.' This is true only if he has a lot of methadone in him."

Gradually, smaller and smaller doses of methadone are given. The patient is finally free of drugs. But in the time he is in treatment, he is getting ready to re-enter society. And he makes it not as a "former addict" but as a whole person, thanks to Patrick House.

PASSAGE 41 QUESTIONS

Directions: If the sentence is true, circle **True**. If the sentence is false, circle **False**.

(D) **1.** No matter how an addict feels about his habit, he has as good a chance as any other addict to kick his habit at Patrick House. True False

(D) **2.** A chief reason Patrick House is so successful is that its workers care about their patients. True False

(D) **3.** Patrick House helps an addict with job skills and medical problems, but does not go into problems of schooling. True False

(D) **4.** Because methadone does not give an addict a "high," it often fails to help him "kick" the habit. True False

(D) **5.** If an addict has any methadone in him, he won't get a "high" with heroin. True False

Directions: Complete these statements.

(SM) **6.** This article is all about ______________________________

(G) **7.** The three most important reasons for the success of Patrick House are:

1. ______________________________
2. ______________________________
3. ______________________________

Directions: Which choice best completes the thought? Circle the letter.

(C) **8.** After reading about Patrick House, it would seem that we could feel that

A. "once an addict, always an addict."
B. if an addict will take a methadone program, he is sure to "make it" in society.
C. addicts can hope to overcome their habit.
D. helping addicts is a simple matter.

42

Fussy people often have a good reason for liking their food or drink "just so." But most of the time their fussiness is just based on a desire to be "with it." Usually, they are imitating someone higher than themselves on the social ladder.

When I was a student, I worked at a hotel during the summer vacations. One man I was serving always ordered a steak for dinner. "Mind you," he would say, "I must have it well done." But no matter how well done the steak was when I brought it, he'd always say, "Take it back and grill it just a little more." One night I took the steak and hid behind a pillar in the dining room. Two minutes later I gave him the steak. "Now *that's* well done," he said. "It's that little extra grilling that makes the difference between a good steak and a great one."

At another time I worked tending bar. Any bartender will tell you there are "in" drinks. At the time, the "in" drink was Chivas Regal scotch. Fussy customers always said "Put it on the rocks, with a twist." A "twist," of course, was a bit of lemon peel to give it that extra something.

Up to my ears with these phonies, I decided to see how good their taste really was. When I got an order of "Chivas, on the rocks, with a twist," I put rye or bourbon in the glass. Not one noticed the change. And my, "Yes sir, you've got it" got me the same tips as if I had served the real thing.

PASSAGE 42 QUESTIONS

Directions: Circle the letter of the choice that best completes each thought below.

(G) **1.** The man who ordered a steak

A. could never be satisfied.
B. really had good taste when it came to steak.
C. was one of the writer's favorite guests.
D. was fooled by the writer.

(G) **2.** The author talks about a "twist" to

A. show how phony some drinkers are.
B. show how some drinkers follow the crowd.
C. show the fine points of drinking.
D. make his example very real to the reader.

(SM) **3.** The subject matter of this passage is

A. people who often have a good reason to be fussy.
B. people who are fussy without good reason.
C. people who drink a lot.
D. student waiters.

Directions: Complete this statement.

(G) **4.** The author gives two stories to prove his belief. He believes that

____

____

43

Primitive man would, the story goes, eat the heart of animals he killed. He would eat the heart of a lion to gain the lion's courage.

"Superstition," you may say. Well, listen to this from the world of science. Dr. Georges Ungar of Baylor University in Houston says that learned information can be passed to other animals from the ones who did the learning.

Dr. Ungar trained rats to prefer lighted boxes to dark boxes. How did he do this to rats that usually prefer the dark? He shocked any rat who went into a dark area. After five to eight days the rats learned that a more peaceful life could be lived in lighted boxes. They got to love the light.

Then he killed the rats. He injected part of their trained brains into 638 mice. These mice had shown they liked the dark. He put parts of the brains of untrained rats into 132 other mice. These mice also liked the dark.

Result? Animals that got the trained brain spent an average of 63 seconds in the dark. Animals that got the untrained brains averaged 118 seconds in the dark.

The figures are very important. Normally only one mouse out of 5,000 would choose the light by chance.

Maybe eating the heart of a lion might not be a bad idea!

PASSAGE 43 QUESTIONS

Directions: If the sentence is true, circle **True**. If the sentence is false, circle **False**.

(D) **1.** Rats prefer the dark. True False

(D) **2.** Dr. Ungar got his rats to prefer the light by keeping their cages under light. True False

(D) **3.** He injected part of the brains of untrained rats into 132 mice. True False

(D) **4.** Mice that got the trained brain spent more time in the dark than mice that got the untrained brain. True False

(D) **5.** Mice, unlike rats, normally prefer the light. True False

Directions: Answer these questions.

(SM) **6.** How would you describe the subject of this passage? This passage is mainly about: ______________________________

____

(G) **7.** What did Dr. Ungar seem to prove? ______________________________

____

(C) **8.** If what he proved is true, what could this mean to people, if there were a way to do it? ______________________________

____

44

Do defensive players prefer a ball carrier to try to get around them or to go through them? Jim Brown put this choice to the Steelers' linemen. They all agreed they would prefer Jim to run *at* them. "This figures," said Jim. "As a runner, I don't feel I have to run *into* tacklers. I don't feel that if I drop a shoulder and hit them with all my force and knock them on their backs or carry them five yards that they are so fainthearted that the next time I come their way, they are going to step aside. You don't hurt a defensive man when you hit him. You hurt him more when he misses you. His job is to stop you and when he comes up empty, that is where the pain is. He's got to answer for that one. It's his job."

PASSAGE 44 QUESTIONS

Directions: Which choice best completes each thought? Circle the letter.

(D) **1.** The Steelers' linemen

A. try to avoid ball carriers.
B. like ball carriers to run at them.
C. are fainthearted.
D. are knocked on their backs when Jim hits them.

(D) **2.** Jim Brown feels that

A. linemen would lose their job if he ran around them.
B. it does not pay to run into tacklers.
C. once he hits a lineman, that man will step aside next time.
D. his idea about ball-carrying disagrees with what the linemen think.

Directions: Complete these statements.

(SM) **3.** This passage is mainly about ______________________________

(G) **4.** The passage backs up the idea that

____

(D) **5.** Two proofs are given to back up the main thought of the passage. These are:

A. What ____________________ said.

B. What ____________________ said.

45

When Muhammad Ali started to push thirty, he knew he was slowing down. He wasn't the fighter he used to be in his early twenties. Soon, he'd be too old to fight. Jack Dempsey had to quit the ring when he turned twenty-nine. Gene Tunney ("The Professor") got out of the boxing game before he was twenty-eight. Joe Louis was a terror in his early twenties. He barely saved his reputation by leaving the ring on his thirty-second birthday. A fighter in his late twenties loses his instant timing. Soon his legs tire after a few rounds. And his punch doesn't pack the old power it had when he was young.

PASSAGE 45 QUESTIONS

Directions: Answer these questions.

(D) **1.** How many great fighters does the passage talk about? ________

(D) **2.** What was said in the passage about every one of these fighters?

____

____

(SM) **3.** What is the writer really talking about? (Circle the letter.)

A. a number of heavyweight champions
B. the fight game
C. how fighters end up when they get old
D. boxing and age

(G) **4.** What is the writer trying to prove?

____

(D) **5.** To back up his GENERAL STATEMENT, what proof does the writer give that has to do with a fighter's body?

____

____

46

The two men started at 4 A.M. The way led from Camp V, at 28,720 feet, to the top. The last 300 feet led up a steep, narrow ridge. For eight hours they clawed their way up the ice. Winds of 110 miles an hour tore at them. First roaring gusts; then eerie silence. They were on oxygen. But each step was supreme effort. Shortly after 12 noon on June 2, 1953, Edmund Hillary and Tenzing Norkay, his Sherpa guide, pulled themselves to the top of the world—Mount Everest.

A newsman had climbed part of the way up with Hillary's party. When Hillary came down, the newsman asked him, "Why did you do it?"

"Because," said the tall New Zealander, "it was there."

Twelve years later, Edmund Hillary took another crack at what made him try the risky climb. He wrote a book about his life. In it he said: "You don't have to be a far-out hero to do great things. You can be an ordinary chap. The main thing is—how much do you *want* to do it? I never liked the danger of climbing. But danger makes you give—give everything you've got. And that—strangely enough—is a very pleasant feeling."

PASSAGE 46 QUESTIONS

Questions: Write the answer to this question.

(D) **1.** What did Edmund Hillary and Tenzing Norkay succeed in doing?

____

Directions: Which choice best completes each thought? Circle the letter.

(D) **2.** On their final climb to the top of Mount Everest, the two men . . . . (You may circle more than one letter.)

A. had bad footing.
B. ran out of oxygen.
C. battled winds.
D. went up 300 feet.

(SM) **3.** In this passage Hillary tries to explain

A. what climbing Everest meant to him.
B. why he wrote his book.
C. why ordinary people can become heroes.
D. how pleasant danger is.

(G) **4.** Hillary's first reason for making the climb (Paragraph 2) could mean

A. really nothing.
B. that Everest was a challenge.
C. that Mount Everest happened to be near where Hillary was climbing.
D. that Hillary wanted to puzzle the newsman.

(G) **5.** Hillary says that the real reason he made the climb was that

A. it was dangerous.
B. he was an ordinary chap.
C. it made him give everything he had.
D. he wanted to do it.

47

1. In one way of thinking, failure is part of life. In another
way, failure may be a way towards success. The "spider-story"
2. is often told. Robert Bruce, leader of the Scots in the 13th
century, was hiding in a cave from the English. He watched a
spider spinning a web. The spider tried to reach across a rough
place in the rock. He tried six times to span the gap. On the
seventh time he made it and went on to spin his web. Bruce is
said to have taken heart and to have gone on to defeat the
English. . . . Edison, the inventor of the light bulb, made
3. hundreds of models that failed before he found the right way to
make one.

---

4. So what? First, always think about your failure. What caused it? Were conditions right? Were you in top form yourself? What can you change so things will go right next time?

---

5. Second, is the goal you're trying to reach the right one? Try to do some thinking about what your real goals may be. Think about this question, "If I do succeed in this, where will it get me?" This may help you prevent failure in things you shouldn't be doing anyway.

---

6. The third thing to bear in mind about failure is that it's a part of life. Learn to "live with yourself" even though you may have failed. Remember, "You can't win 'em all."

PASSAGE 47 QUESTIONS

Directions: Which choice best completes the thought? Circle the letter.

(SM) **1.** This passage deals with two sides of failure. In Section 1 the author talks mainly about

A. the value of failure.
B. how people fail.
C. famous failures.
D. how not to fail.

Directions: Complete this statement.

(SM) **2.** In Section 2 the author talks mainly about

____

Directions: Circle the letter of the choice that best completes each thought below.

(G) **3.** Robert Bruce was put in the passage to show that

A. failure must come before success.
B. failure isn't all bad.
C. nature will help us if we let it.
D. people who fail have plenty of company.

(G) **4.** One thing the writer does **not** tell you to do to cope with failure is:

A. check out your goals to see if they are right for you.
B. think about failure as part of life.
C. think about a failure to find out what went wrong.
D. avoid things that are beyond you.

48

1. Sumo wrestling goes back to olden times in Japan. Early sumo bouts were held at Shinto shrines to bring rain. In those days there were no rules. Defeat often meant death. But over the years rules were made and customs grew up. Today *sumatori* (the wrestlers), judges, referees, and trainers all follow these rules and customs.

---

2. One thing that has also grown over the years is the size of the wrestlers. The sumatori are big men. A lad who tips in at 225 is small. Many weigh 300 pounds; some, over that. Some look as if they carry some lard. But most of it's muscle, with enough flesh to cushion the bumps.

---

3. All a wrestler wears is a belt—called a *mawashi*—that is wrapped around the waist and between the legs. Years ago mawashi were dark-colored, but today they come in all colors from baby blue to orange.

PASSAGE 48 QUESTIONS

Directions: Circle the letter of the choice that best completes each thought below.

(G) **1.** Sumo wrestling
- A. has a long history.
- B. is done to bring rain.
- C. has freed itself of the many rules it used to have.
- D. is today part of the Shinto faith.

(G) **2.** The sumo wrestlers are
- A. flabby.
- B. large, but flabby.
- C. large and strong.
- D. not as large as they used to be.

Directions: Give a title for each section of this passage:

(SM) **3.** Section 1: ______________________________

Section 2: ______________________________

Section 3: ______________________________

As you watch a sumo match, you see the customs that have grown up with the years. First the junior wrestlers come in and hold their matches. Then, around three in the afternoon, the senior men parade. Each wrestler wears his *kehomawashi* — a heavy apron with sewed-on pictures, costing a thousand dollars.

Then come the *yokozuna* — the grand champions of sumo. There are only two or three of these at any one time. The five or six hundred men in sumo are broken up into seven classes. Each yokozuna has worked his way up through these seven grades. To be yokozuna is to be a Babe Ruth or a Hank Aaron. Here fame brings fortune. The fans bring him gifts. And he makes a bundle each time he wrestles.

When a yokozuna steps into the ring, wrapped in his white robe, a singing hum rises from the fans. He has with him a handler, and a sword bearer. These men sit without moving. The yokozuna goes through his postures. Then the referee — in a bright kimono — steps in. He carries his badge of office — a paddle with a long tassel.

These customs go on through the day. Each wrestler washes his mouth before a bout. Then he throws salt into the ring to clean the area of combat. He claps his hands to call the gods. He raises his arms to show that he has no weapons. If he loses, he bows before he leaves the ring. If he wins, he squats to hear his name sung out. He blesses the money on the referee's paddle. Only then does he take it.

PASSAGE 49 QUESTIONS

(SM) **1.** Show in what order these items appear in the passage. (Put the right letters on the blank lines.)

A. Senior men parade. 1. ________
B. Wrestlers call on the gods. 2. ________
C. Referee wears a bright kimono. 3. ________
D. Junior men come in. 4. ________
E. Winner takes the money. 5. ________
F. Fans greet the champions with a singing hum. 6. ________

(G) **2.** If you think about this passage as a whole, the main point about sumo wrestling seems to be that

A. the wrestlers wear expensive clothes.
B. they take a long time.
C. sumo wrestlers are very organized, like a union.
D. custom, tradition, and even religion are part of it.

50

The rules of sumo wrestling are simple. The ring is round. Is is formed by a rope sunk in clay. Once the fight is on, the wrestler wins by forcing the other man to go outside the rope. He can also win if he can get his rival to touch the clay floor with any part of his body other than his feet.

It's a one-fall match. It may go faster than the Joe Louis-Max Schmelling bout of 1938—in which Louis won in 7 seconds. A side-step to dodge the opening charge, a clop on the back, and a fighter wins as his rival goes down in the clay. Other times a match may go four minutes as two evenly-matched men work to gain leverage on each other's belt.

During the bout the wrestler may strike with his open hand. He may trip but not kick. He may push. But he cannot grab the hair or the throat to choke. He may grab the belt anywhere in the middle but not below the waist.

PASSAGE 50 QUESTIONS

Directions: Complete these statements.

(G) **1.** Two ways a sumo wrestler can win are:

A. ______________________________

B. ______________________________

(D) **2.** Three things the sumo wrestler may not do are:

A. ______________________________

B. ______________________________

C. ______________________________

Directions: Which choice best completes each thought? Circle the letter.

(G) **3.** A sumo match can last

A. no set length of time.
B. not more than four minutes.
C. seven seconds.
D. between seven seconds and four minutes.

(SM) **4.** This part of the Sumo Wrestling story concentrates on

A. the dangers to the wrestlers.
B. the length of the match.
C. the rules of sumo.
D. how a wrestler wins at sumo.

51

The moves in sumo are the thing to watch. There are two types of fighters. The "thrusters" use their great weight and strength to shove their rivals off balance. The "grapplers" go for the belt. They try to win by arm throws.

Jessie Takanohana, a trim but strong *ozeki*—champion—goes for the belt. He's smaller than most, so his only hope is to get a hold on his rival's belt. Jesse has at least twelve different armthrows. It's great to watch Takanohana come out of his first charge with his legs crouched and his arms slashing away at his rival.

The prettiest of Takanohana's moves is his *utchari*. It is a last-second try to snatch victory from defeat. It comes when he has been shoved back to the edge of the ring by the weight of a bigger man. There, Takanohana plants his feet, heels on the rope. Every muscle in his thick legs strains to lift the other man by his belt. Then using the pushing of the other man, he twists at the very last moment and tips him off balance. If Jesse makes it, his rival hits the clay first as they go crashing out of the ring.

PASSAGE 51 QUESTIONS

Directions: Complete these statements.

(G) **1.** In sumo, fighters fall into two types: A, those who try to

____

and B, those who try to win by ________________________

____

(G) **2.** Jesse Takanohana tries to win by . . . (Circle the letter.)

A. slashing at his rival.
B. using one of twelve armthrows.
C. using his weight to throw rivals off balance.
D. allowing himself to be pushed back to the rope.

(SIG) **3.** A good title for this fourth part of the Sumo story might be

____

52

Have you ever had a steaming dish of spaghetti, say, with a spicy tomato sauce? Or better yet, with a rich, chewy meat sauce? It's a great dish, and it shows what can be done with the lowly noodle—which is, of course, what spaghetti is made from. We owe this tasty dish to the magic worked with the noodle over the centuries by Italian cooks.

In Italy the noodle is a form of *pasta.* Pasta is made from the semolina milled from durum wheat—a hard, flinty plant, rich in gluten and protein. Sometimes the pasta dough is enriched with eggs, or even spinach, to give it flavor. It can be served boiled, with sauce, like spaghetti, or baked like lasagna. It can be stuffed with meat, cheese, or other fillings like ravioli or tortelini. And it is usually served sprinkled with grated cheese.

Pasta comes in more than sixty shapes. The three main forms are tubular, such as spaghetti and macaroni; flat, such as fettucini and lasagna, or small grains, such as soup-pasta. The pastas vary from very thin tubes (vermicelli) to large sheets (lasagna). The names of the types of pasta tell their shapes. *Cannelloni* are big pipes. *Cappeletti* are little hats. *Ochi di lapo* are wolves' eyes, *quadrucci* are little squares, and *vermicelli* are little worms. The word *spaghetti* comes from *spago*, a string.

Marco Polo gets the credit for bringing pasta to Venice, Italy, seven hundred years ago. But another story gives the nod to the German tribes who invaded Italy in the fifth century. A handsome Italian soldier is said to have won the love of a tribal chief's kitchen maid. He pried the secret of noodle-making from her and passed it on to his grateful countrymen. Since the fifth century Italians all over the world have never been able to get enough of their beloved pasta.

PASSAGE 52 QUESTIONS

Directions: This passage tells you about pasta. In it, different sides of the pasta story are told. Divide the passage up into sections.

(SM) **1.** Draw a line from the left margin to the right margin through the the passage to show where one section ends and the next one begins.

(SM) Number each section. Put a 1, 2, 3, 4, etc. beside each section.

(SM) For each of your sections, show by a short title what part of the pasta story is told in that section. To start you off, a title for the first section is filled in.

Section No.	**Title**
1	*"The noodle's appeal"*
2	________________
3	________________
4	________________
5	________________

Directions: Complete these sentences.

(G) **2.** Spaghetti, lasagna, and macaroni are all forms of __________ .

(D) **3.** You can add __________ or __________ to pasta dough to give it more flavor.

(D) **4.** Pasta can be served baked, or __________, or __________ .

53

When, after a year of being alone on his island, Robinson Crusoe sees a footprint in the sand, the reader of *Robinson Crusoe* trembles. Will Crusoe find another human being to end his loneliness? Is the footprint the sign of an enemy? Since 1719, when Daniel Defoe wrote *Robinson Crusoe*, thousands of people who enjoy English novels have thrilled to this great adventure story. But few know how the story came to be written. Robinson Crusoe was the first English novel. Its birth brought together the misadventures of a Scotch "failure" and the untapped imagination of an aging English scribbler.

Near the end of the Seventeenth Century, the hot-tempered Alexander Selkirk was charged with bad conduct while in church. Rather than face this charge, he ran away to sea. Several years later, Selkirk found himself on the ship of an English privateer. The privateer was preying on Spanish shipping. But Selkirk quarreled bitterly with the Captain. So, when the ship came to the island of Juan Fernandez in the South Seas, Selkirk asked to be put ashore. When he saw that there were no people on the island, he begged to be taken back on board. But the Captain refused—Selkirk had gone too far. Over four years later, Selkirk was rescued by another ship.

When Selkirk got back to England, the story of his life on the island fired the imagination of Daniel Defoe. Defoe had been earning a living by his pen since he was thirty. He was amazingly hard-working. He wrote a whole newspaper three times a week. He also made part of his living from politics. He supported both political parties. He told each party that it had his sole support.

Defoe's morals were weak. But he was a fine writer. He was almost sixty when, in the midst of his work in politics, he wrote *Robinson Crusoe.* In it, Defoe—said one critic—"forged a story, and forced it on the world for truth." The detail of Crusoe's battle for survival on a lonely island is so vivid that the reader of *Robinson Crusoe* accepts the product of the author's imagination for reality. Robinson Crusoe became the first of a long line of heroes and heroines that have peopled English novels since Defoe's time.

PASSAGE 53 QUESTIONS

Directions: Which choice best completes each thought? Circle the letter.

(D) **1.** Alexander Selkirk spent four years on a desert island because

A. he sought adventure.
B. he was hot-tempered.
C. he was afraid to face charges.
D. his ship was wrecked.

(D) **2.** Daniel Defoe

A. made his living as a writer.
B. got his start as a writer with the writing of *Robinson Crusoe.*
C. was very "straight"—he was hardworking and honest.
D. had little power of imagination, but succeeded with his novel because he worked hard.

(SM) **3.** This passage answers the question,

A. How was Alexander Selkirk able to survive on the island?
B. Why do people enjoy English novels?
C. What did the footprint in the sand mean?
D. How did *Robinson Crusoe* come to be written?

Directions: Circle **True** or **False** for each sentence.

(G) **4.** *Robinson Crusoe* was a successful novel. True False

(G) **5.** Even if Alexander Selkirk had not lived on the island of Juan Fernandez, *Robinson Crusoe* would still have been written. True False

(G) **6.** Daniel Defoe lived partly by hard work and partly by "his wits." True False

(G) **7.** With the writing of *Robinson Crusoe*, the English novel was born. True False

54

1. Some time ago, while traveling in Japan, I was asked to come to a firewalking at *Shimei-in.* Shimei-in is a temple in the hills of Kyoto, in Japan. At the temple, the fire of logs had burned down. As it burned the priests had chanted prayers. They had blown on conch shells. They had covered the logs with evergreen branches. The coals were raked out. The coals made a path about twenty feet long. And now the firewalking was to begin.

Go on to next page. ➤

The chief priest, in a robe of red and purple, steps out to face the coals. He pours salt over them. He stands still and prays to himself. He gets himself together. The heat of the coals rolls out at him. Then, slowly, firmly, he walks barefoot the length of the glowing path. Then he turns and waits.

---

2. The other *yamabushi*—men of the order—follow, by rank. Then non-members walk the coals. Young and old, men, women and children, businessmen and fishermen, students and shopkeepers, all walk across. As they walk, they chant a Buddhist prayer. The coals are red underneath, dull-black on top.

Now it is my turn. My friend, a Tokyo businessman, says, "C'mon, let's go." He walks across, hands folded, eyes ahead, chanting. His broad, bare feet roll over the coals.

---

3. For some reason, I thought of a movie I saw a long time ago. One scene had stayed with me. A woman bent over candles that lit the room. One by one, she snuffed them out between her thumb and her forefinger. As each candle went out, she smiled. . . . The secret of firewalking is confidence. Did I have it? I followed my friend across. But halfway over the path of coals, I knew I wouldn't make it. Pain. And blisters.

---

4. I lived in Japan for ten years after that first failure to firewalk. I read up on firewalking. It's done in many places in the East.

In Fiji a pit is filled with rocks. These are heated for six hours, to a heat of 1,800 degrees. They are then walked on. In Ceylon, men, women, and children dance on coals whose heat may reach 1,328 degrees.

How do they do it? "Faith, total faith in our gods." In the villages where this is done prayers and other sacred rites go on for three months. In Japan they rake out the coals. But in Fiji and Ceylon the coals are kept in a trench. It keeps the heat in and makes the coals hotter.

Dr. Leonard Feinberg of Iowa State College was at the festival of the god Katarajama in Ceylon in 1956. The bonfire burned for four hours. Of the 80 people who walked over it, 12 went to the hospital and one died.

5. Later, in Japan, I was able to walk over the coals, not once but four times.

What's the secret? How can people brave the fierce heat? I keep thinking of the actress who smiled as she snuffed out the candles. Confidence. Of course, the ritual, the prayers, the concentration help confidence. And so does the thought that the gods protect you. The Japanese say that, to master the fire, you must first master yourself.

---

6. Firewalking is a test. Those who trust in themselves and in the natural world about them seem to make it across the coals unharmed.

PASSAGE 54 QUESTIONS

Directions: Complete these sentences.

(SM) **1.** Section 1 deals with firewalking at ______________________ .

(SM) **2.** Section 4 deals with firewalking in ______________________ .

Directions: Circle **True** or **False**.

(D) **3.** It is best to keep quiet when walking across the coals, in order to keep your mind on what you are doing. True False

(D) **4.** The actress the author thought about felt no pain when she put out the candles. True False

(D) **5.** In Fiji and Ceylon, even though the fire was much hotter than in Japan, all the people who firewalked were successful. True False

(G) **6.** At Shimei-in and in Fiji, firewalking is part of the religion. True False

(G) **7.** If we believe the author, firewalking was no problem for him. True False

Directions: Which choice best completes the thought? Circle the letter.

(G) **8.** The article makes the point that firewalking success is

A. a physical ability.
B. a mental matter.
C. an unexplained happening.
D. an ability you've either got or you haven't—and if you haven't, nothing can be done about it.

55

Many famous people, it seems, come out of nowhere. They appear, they "do their thing," they become known overnight. And that's that.

Or is it?

Take Robert Fulton. On Monday, August 17, 1807, Fulton startled the world. He had made a steamboat that worked.

He had named his boat the *Clermont*. It was to go from New York City to Albany—150 miles. The morning of that day Fulton's boat was at a dock on the Hudson River in New York. After moving a short way from the dock the boat stopped. The twenty-four people on the boat thought it wouldn't work. They were having second thoughts about going. Fulton went below. He fixed the engine.

The *Clermont* got to Albany on Wednesday. By Friday, Fulton and his boat were back at the dock in New York. In one week Robert Fulton had made a place for himself in the history books.

But the *Clermont* wasn't Fulton's first try at fame and fortune. Ever since he was a young man he had been interested in new ideas for things. He worked on an idea for a marble-cutting machine. He thought up a way to raise canal boats from one level to another, without locks. And then he got an idea for a submarine. An underwater ship, Fulton thought, could place a bomb under a ship and blow it up.

Fulton was living in Europe. So he wrote to Napoleon. "I will pay to build my submarine," he wrote, "if you will pay for each British ship I sink."

Fulton got the sub built in the summer of 1802. He called it the *Nautilus*. It worked fine on the Seine River in Paris. The sub went under for twenty minutes, then came up. The people on the banks cheered. The torpedo idea worked out also. While Napoleon's Navy officers watched, Fulton blew up an old ship in the harbor of Brest.

Then Fulton tried to blow up two British ships blocking a French harbor. Fulton, in the *Nautilus*, got as close to the ships as he dared. Then he took it down. The four men in the sub had to crank the paddle wheels by hand. They moved slowly. While they were down in the dark water the British ships set sail! So Napoleon didn't buy the torpedo idea.

But Fulton kept trying. When he saw he couldn't sell the sub idea, he turned to the idea of a steamboat. As early as 1803, Robert Livingston had asked Fulton to build a steamboat. Livingston was the U.S. ambassador to France. He had a place on the Hudson River, named Clermont. The steamboat would sail the Hudson.

When he set to work on a steamboat, Fulton was still in Europe. He worked long and hard at it. He went over the plans of a boat built in Scotland. He studied other boats. Then he added changes. He tried his boat out on the Seine. It was O.K. Later, when Fulton built the *Clermont* in America, he made more changes, up to the last day before it steamed up the Hudson.

PASSAGE 55 QUESTIONS

Directions: Circle **True** or **False**.

(G) **1.** Fulton's trip up the Hudson to Albany was a surprise to most people. True False

(G) **2.** The twenty-four people Fulton took on the trip never lost their faith in him. True False

(G) **3.** Fulton worked on many other inventions before he built his steamboat. True False

(G) **4.** But when he built the *Clermont*, he did it easily, with few changes and little previous study. True False

Directions: Which choice best completes the thought? Circle the letter.

(G) **5.** This writer seems to feel that people who become famous "overnight" become so because

A. of one amazing feat.
B. they worked hard and long before.
C. they try their hands at many things until one "clicks."
D. of whom they know.

56

We always wonder about famous people. What were they really like?

Sigmund Freud, the world-famous doctor of Vienna, was a thinker who changed the way we look at mental trouble. He was also a man with guts.

Once Freud was walking down a dark street. He was met by two toughs who wanted to mug him. This was back in 1890. Freud took his cane by the tip and beat off the muggers.

He did not lose his cool when the Nazis came to his house. The Nazi soldiers found 1500 shillings (about $250) in a drawer. Their sergeant put the money in his pocket. He wrote out a receipt, clicked his heels, and was about to leave. "You're very lucky," said Dr. Freud.

"Why?" asked the young sergeant.

"Well," said the Professor, as he was called, "I've been a doctor here in Vienna for 40 years, and I never got 1500 shillings for just one visit."

Freud had guts. He also had a sense of humor. Once, at his 70th birthday party, a relative asked Freud if he could put his work into simple words. "Well," said the Professor, "we take the patient out of his mental trouble, and return him to the common misery."

Freud had three sisters. They had never married. They each lived in a small apartment. Freud and his brother paid the sisters' bills. The sisters lived simply. The brother asked Uncle Sigi (as Freud was called in his large family) if the sisters could live together. "It's logical," said the brother, "it would save money."

Freud said, "Yes, it's logical, but it wouldn't be psychological." The sisters kept their own apartments, and the idea was dropped.

Freud was a devoted son. His mother used to spend her summers in Ischl, a small mountain town in Austria. The Emperor Franz Josef used to spend his summers in Ischl, too.

Grandma Freud, as she was called by the family, used to sit at the window and watch the crowds on Main Street. Freud was visiting his mother on her 95th birthday. The band was playing a lively tune. The old lady's memory must have failed her. She heard the band playing, but forgot it was the Emperor's birthday. The professor told his mother, "Mama, the band is playing for your birthday." She believed him and had a wonderful day.

PASSAGE 56 QUESTIONS

Directions: Which choice best completes each thought? Circle the letter.

(G) **1.** The writer tells about how Freud used his cane to show

A. how unsafe the streets were in Freud's time.
B. that it was normal to carry a cane.
C. that Freud was brave.
D. that there was poor lighting in the streets in Vienna.

(G) **2.** The author tells what Freud said to the Nazi sergeant to show that he

A. was not afraid of the Nazis.
B. had a sense of humor.
C. was making out as a doctor.
D. did not care about money.

(G) **3.** Freud did not ask his sisters to live together because

A. it would not be cheaper.
B. his brother's logic was wrong.
C. they might not get along.
D. he had plenty of money to support them.

(G) **4.** The author tells how Freud lied to his mother to show that he

A. had a flaw in his make-up.
B. felt it didn't matter what he said to his mother because she was so old.
C. didn't like the Emperor.
D. liked his mother very much.

Directions: Complete this statement.

(SM) **5.** A good title for this passage might be ______________________________

____

57

Do you sometimes argue about what seems to you to be simple fact? Do you argue about whether it's cold outdoors or whether the car in front of you is going faster than the speed limit?

If you get into such arguments, try to think about the six blind men and the elephant in the Sultan's court.

The Sultan was fond of puzzles, so he had six blind men brought in and allowed them to feel his prize elephant. "What manner of beast is this creature?" asked the Sultan.

"O Sultan," said the first blind man, who had felt the elephant's trunk, "it is like a snake."

"O Great One," said the second man, who had felt the elephant's side, "it is like a living wall."

"O Learned One," said the third, who had gripped a tusk, "it seems to be as hard as ivory."

The fourth man, who had hold of the tail, thought that the animal was soft like a brush; while the fifth, who had put his hand near the mouth, thought it was like a big fish. The sixth man, who had got hold of an ear, felt that the beast was like a soft carpet.

Each man's idea of the animal came from his own experience. So if someone disagrees with you about a "simple fact," it's often because his experience in the matter is different from yours.

To see how hard it is for even *one* person to make up his mind about a "simple fact," try this simple experiment. Get three large bowls. Put ice water in one. Put hot water in the second. Put lukewarm water in the third. Now put your left hand in the ice water. Put your right hand in the hot water. After thirty seconds, put both hands in the lukewarm water. Your right hand will tell you the water is cold. Your left hand will tell you it's hot!

PASSAGE 57 QUESTIONS

Directions: Circle the letter of the choice that best completes each thought below.

(D) **1.** The six blind men said what they did because they

A. wanted to please the Sultan.
B. wanted to argue with each other.
C. had never heard of an elephant.
D. went by what they felt with their hands.

(D) **2.** If you do the experiment with the bowls of water, you will find that

A. the water will feel lukewarm.
B. your hands are "lying" to you.
C. water can have two temperatures at the same time.
D. none of the above is true.

Directions: Complete these statements.

(SM) **3.** This passage is mainly about

____

____

(G) **4.** The author tries to show that

____

____

____

Directions: Which choice best completes the thought? Circle the letter.

(C) **5.** In deciding about "simple" facts, it would seem to be smart to

A. go by what you think is right.
B. go by what someone else says.
C. think about how your experience might mislead you.
D. never decide anything because you'll always be wrong.

58

South of Jerusalem, near the Dead Sea, the land is harsh. Here is desert sand, huge rocky hills, dry, worn-out *wadis.* In a cave in these forbidding hills, a shepherd boy found the first Dead Sea Scroll in a clay jar in 1947. As Israeli scholars learned of the scroll, they followed the trail of the shepherd boy into the desert. The caves were hard to find, and harder to get into. At one of the caves in the side of a cliff—the "Cave of the Vulture"—the searchers had to swing from ropes into the mouth of the cave. After twenty years of detective work and risky, costly trips to the desert, the scholars now have all the scrolls in a special building in Jerusalem.

What are the "Dead Sea Scrolls"? The scrolls themselves were rolled up sheets made of leather (parchment) and of papyrus. Leather was used for religious writing. Papyrus—the "paper" of the ancient world—was used for other writing.

And why did the scholars risk life and limb to find them? The scrolls were books written by a small sect of Jews known as the Essenes over 2,000 years ago. They tell us what people thought and did at the time that Jesus walked the hills of the Holy Land. At that time the Holy Land was called Judea.

PASSAGE 58 QUESTIONS

Directions: Write out the answers to the following questions:

(G) **1.** WHERE were the Dead Sea Scrolls found?

____

____

(G) **2.** WHO were the people who had something to do with finding them?

____

____

(G) **3.** WHEN were they found?

____

(G) **4.** HOW did the scholars get at them?

____

____

(G) **5.** WHAT are the scrolls?

____

____

(G) **6.** WHY did the scholars want them?

____

____

59

One of the things the Dead Sea Scrolls tell us about is the writing of the Bible. Before the scrolls, the oldest copies we had of the Bible were written during the Middle Ages—about 700-900 A.D. But many of the scrolls are books of the Bible. And they are very much like the ones written in the Middle Ages! So now we know that the Bible we have today has not been changed for at least 2,000 years.

In some ways life 2,000 years ago wasn't too different. Some of the writings found in the caves of Nahal Hever are about marriage contracts, divorce, and the passing down of wealth from parent to child. One scroll tells of the troubles of a rich woman, Babta Bat Shimon. She owned houses and land. She also had two husbands. The scroll tells of the arguments she had with her husbands—and their families—over the rights to her properties.

Perhaps the most startling find among the Dead Sea Scrolls are the letters of Bar Kochba. Shimon Bar Kochba was the leader of the last revolt of the Jews against the Romans. Until the scrolls were found, Bar Kochba was a legend. But now there is proof that he was a real person. His letters show that he was a stern commander. In one letter he threatens to put chains on the feet of a captain if he does not carry out his orders.

Bar Kochba's men and women fighters were called the Zealots. They rebelled against the Roman aim to crush the Jewish faith all through Judea. The Zealots holed up in the desert caves. As the Romans pressed in on all sides, the Zealots made their final stand in a rocky fortress known as Masada. For a year the Zealots held out. Finally, the Romans built a huge ramp into the fort. But when the Roman soldiers burst into Masada, they found all the defenders dead. As Josephus, a Roman writer said: ". . . . The Romans did not celebrate their victory, as is the custom. Rather they stood amazed at this deed, carried out by all in utter contempt of death. . . ."

Today, the Dead Sea Scrolls are under glass in the "Shrine of the Book," a special building in Jerusalem. Pictures have been taken of them, and books with what they say have been printed. They are living history, open to all.

PASSAGE 59 QUESTIONS

Directions: Complete these statements.

(G) **1.** Because we have the Scrolls, we now know that some of the books of the Bible we use really go back at least ________ years.

(SM) **2.** Paragraph 2 of this passage deals with

____

____

2000 years ago.

(G) **3.** It uses the examples of the rich woman, Babta Bat Shimon, to show us that 2000 years ago, people

____

____

just as they do today.

(SM) **4.** Paragraph 3 deals with

____

(G) **5.** The main thing it tells us is that

____

(SM) **6.** This passage tells us what we learned from the Dead Sea Scrolls. What two topics did we learn about?

____

____

60

Have you ever been afraid to talk back when you were treated unfairly? Have you ever bought something just because the salesman talked you into it? Are you afraid to ask someone for a date?

Many people are afraid to assert themselves. Dr. Robert Alberti, author of *Stand Up, Speak Out, and Talk Back*, thinks it's because their self-esteem is low. "Our whole set-up is geared to make people distrust themselves," says Alberti. "There's always a 'superior' around—a parent, a teacher, a boss—who 'knows better.' These 'superiors' often gain when they chip away at your self-image."

But Alberti and other scientists are doing something to help people assert themselves. They offer "assertiveness training" courses—AT for short. In the AT course people learn that they have a right to be themselves. They learn to speak out and feel good about doing so. They learn to be aggressive without hurting other people.

In one way, learning to speak out is to overcome fear. A group taking an AT course will help the timid person to lose his fear. But AT uses an even stronger motive—the need to share. The timid person speaks out in the group because he wants to tell how he feels.

Whether or not you speak up for yourself depends on your self-image. If someone you face is more "important" than you, you may feel less of a person. You start to doubt your own good sense. You go by the other person's label. But, why should you? AT says you can get to feel good about yourself. And once you do, you can learn to speak out.

PASSAGE 60 QUESTIONS

Directions: Circle the letter of the choice that best completes each thought below.

(G) **1.** The PROBLEM the writer talks about is that

A. some people buy things they don't want.
B. some people are afraid to stick up for their rights.
C. there are too many "chiefs" and not enough "Indians."
D. some people don't think highly enough of themselves.

(G) **2.** The CAUSE of the PROBLEM talked about in this passage is that

A. some people have a low self-image.
B. there is always someone around who "knows better."
C. salesmen talk people into buying things they don't want.
D. people don't share enough.

(G) **3.** The EFFECT of our "set-up" on people is often to

A. make them distrust their own answers to problems.
B. make things more favorable for "superiors."
C. keep them from knowing as much as their "superiors" know.
D. help them to learn to speak up for their rights.

(G) **4.** AT is one SOLUTION to the PROBLEM in this passage. One thing AT *doesn't* do is

A. use the need of people to share.
B. show people they have a right to be themselves.
C. help people overcome fear.
D. help people to assert themselves even if others suffer.

Directions: Complete this statement.

(SIG) **5.** A good title for this passage could be

____

61

Thirty-two people watched Kitty Genovese being killed right beneath their windows. She was their neighbor. Yet none of the 32 helped her. Not one even called the police. Was this inhuman cruelty? Was it lack of feeling about one's fellow man?

"Not so," say scientists John Darley and Bibb Fatane. These men went beyond the headlines to probe the reasons why people didn't act. They found that a person has to go through two steps before he can help. First he has to notice that there *is* an emergency.

Suppose you see a middle-aged man slump to the sidewalk. Is he having a heart attack? Is he in a coma from diabetes? Or is he about to sleep off a drunk?

Is the smoke coming into the room from a leak in the air conditioning? Is it "steam pipes"? Or is it really smoke from a fire? It's not always easy to tell if you are faced with a real emergency.

Second, and more important, the person faced with an emergency must feel personally responsible. He must feel that he must help, or the person won't get the help he needs.

The researchers found that a lot depends on how many people are around. They had college students in to be "tested." Some came alone. Some came with one or two others. And some came in large groups. The receptionist started them off on the "tests." Then she went into the next room. A curtain divided the "testing room" and the room into which she went. Soon the students heard a scream, the noise of file cabinets falling and a cry for help. All of this had been pre-recorded on a tape-recorder.

Eight out of ten of the students taking the test alone acted to help. Of the students in pairs, only two out of ten helped. Of the students in groups, none helped.

In other words, in a group, Americans often fail to act. They feel that others will act. They, themselves, needn't. They do not feel any direct responsibility.

Are people bothered by situations where people are in trouble? Yes. The scientists found that the people were emotional, they sweated, they had trembling hands. They felt the other person's trouble. But they did not act. They were in a group. Their actions were shaped by the actions of those they were with.

PASSAGE 61 QUESTIONS

Directions: Which choice best completes each thought? Circle the letter.

(D) **1.** Suppose you see a middle-age man slump to the sidewalk. Of the following, which could be true?

A. The man might be in a coma from diabetes.
B. The man is having a heart attack.
C. The man is going to sleep off a drunk.
D. Any of the above.

(D) **2.** When the students heard the "scream" and "the cry for help," the ones who most often acted were

A. taking the tests in groups.
B. taking the tests alone.
C. taking the tests in pairs.
D. not Americans.

(SM) **3.** This passage tries to explain

A. when people will act in emergencies.
B. why people are cruel.
C. how to tell what is an emergency.
D. how science can explain emotions.

Directions: If the sentence is true, circle **True**. If the sentence is false, circle **False.**

(G) **4.** It's easy to tell when there is an emergency. True False

(G) **5.** People by themselves tend to act because by themselves, they feel emotions strongly. True False

(G) **6.** The passage seems to show that people who fail to act in emergencies are not cruel. True False

62

"Keep your eye on the ball." That is good advice when you're at the plate, and good advice for everyday living. "Keep your mind on what's important," is the way I'd put it. But people are funny. They get messed up with the details.

I had a secretary once. She was very hardworking. I ran a school, and people used to call up to enroll for courses. Betty used to get angry at the phone. "If they keep on ringing, I'll never get my typing done!" she'd wail.

People just don't see the big picture. One evening, after leaving work, I was sitting next to a man on the train. I was feeling tired and kind of mellow. My eyes fell on the paper the man was reading. So I started reading the page the man had spread out in front of him. You know how you sort of read over someone's shoulder?

I read the page and leaned back. I guess I was waiting for him to turn it. After a while, I realized—he wasn't turning the page. He just kept on reading.

Now, if you knew the rag he was reading, you'd know that there weren't many words on the page to read anyway. The layout was mostly pictures. So I turned to the man and said, "You know, you really read very slowly."

"What do you mean?" he asked. "Well," I told him, "I read that page in about a minute, and you've taken about ten. And you're still reading. You know," I went on, "if you learned to read faster, you could get more reading done."

He chewed on that for a minute or two. "If I read too fast," he said, finally, "my paper wouldn't last me to my station."

PASSAGE 62 QUESTIONS

Directions: Write the answers to these questions.

(D) **1.** What did the author's secretary think when students called up to enroll in the school?

____

____

(D) **2.** What good would it have done the train rider to be able to read faster?

____

____

Directions: Circle the letter of the choice that best completes each thought below.

(SM) **3.** This passage is really about

A. reading faster.
B. secretaries.
C. people's judgment.
D. impolite authors.

(G) **4.** The author believes that people

A. fail to place the right value on things they do.
B. should not read faster.
C. should apply the rules of baseball to life.
D. are wrong to follow their own beliefs.

Directions: Answer this question.

(SIG) **5.** If you agree with the writer of this passage, what would be a good rule for you to follow?

____

____

63

A moment's drilling by the dentist may make us nervous and upset. Many of us cannot stand pain. To avoid the pain of a drilling that may last perhaps a minute or two, we demand the "needle"—a shot of novocaine—that deadens the nerves around the tooth.

Now it's true that the human body has developed its millions of nerves to be highly aware of what goes on both inside and outside of it. This helps us adjust to the world. Without our nerves—and our brain, which is a bundle of nerves—we wouldn't know what's happening. But we pay for our sensitivity. We can feel pain when the slightest thing is wrong with any part of our body. The history of torture is based on the human body being open to pain.

But there is a way to handle pain. Look at the Indian fakir who sits on a bed of nails. Fakirs can put a needle right through an arm, and feel no pain. This ability that some humans have developed to handle pain should give us ideas about how the mind can deal with pain.

The big thing in withstanding pain is our attitude toward it. If the dentist says, "This will hurt a little," it helps us to accept the pain. By staying relaxed, and by *treating the pain as an interesting sensation*, we can handle the pain without falling apart. After all, although pain is an unpleasant sensation, it is still a sensation, and sensations are the stuff of life.

PASSAGE 63 QUESTIONS

Directions: Circle the letter of the choice that best completes each thought below.

(SM) **1.** The purpose of this passage is mainly to tell us

A. that pain is good for us.
B. to stop taking the "needle" at the dentist's.
C. how to handle pain.
D. how to avoid torture.

(G) **2.** The purpose of pain is to

A. let us know what's going on.
B. make us open to torture.
C. make us pay for our sensitivity.
D. help us get more sensations.

(G) **3.** The most important thing in handling pain is to

A. do what the Indian fakirs do.
B. welcome it.
C. know about it in advance.
D. treat it as an interesting sensation.

64

Paris, July 14, 1789. There was a shortage of corn. The price of bread was higher than it had ever been in living memory. Did the King and his nobles plan to starve the citizens of France in order to force them to give in? Mobs of citizens roamed the streets, seeking arms, trying to get together to fight the government.

Jean-Baptiste Humbert, a watchmaker, tells us in the diary he kept that arms, buckshot, and powder were being given to citizens at the Hotel de Ville. As Humbert left the hotel with his musket and six pellets of buckshot, firing was heard from the direction of the Bastille. A shout went up: "To the Bastille!"

It was half past three when Humbert got to the fortress. The outer drawbridge had already been pulled down by the attackers. Now they were trying to drag two cannon into the outer courtyard. Humbert gave them a hand, and soon found himself in front of the crowd. Just as the cannon were placed at the main gate, the defenders raised the drawbridge. Humbert fired six rounds of ammunition. As he did so, a hand appeared through a small hole in the main gate waving a piece of paper. One of the citizens placed a beam across the moat. A man walked across, seized the note, and read it out loud:

"We have twenty thousand pounds of gunpowder. We will blow up the garrison and the whole district if you do not surrender. The Bastille, 5 p.m., July 14, 1789."

The note was signed by de Launay, commander of the fortress. It didn't work. "Lower the drawbridge! We shall never give in!" were the shouts. The citizens reloaded the cannon. They were about to fire when the drawbridge was suddenly lowered. The soldiers of the garrison had sided with the citizens. They had forced the commander to open the gates. The crowd poured into the Bastille, Humbert in the lead. Nine hundred and fifty-four craftsmen, shopkeepers and common citizens had earned themselves the title, "Conquerors of the Bastille."

PASSAGE 64 QUESTIONS

Directions: Circle the letter of the choice that best completes each thought below.

(G) **1.** French citizens were ready to fight in 1789 because

A. arms were being given out.
B. the nobles had attacked them.
C. they could not get bread or corn.
D. leaders, such as Jean-Baptiste Humbert, had sprung up.

(G) **2.** De Launay surrendered the Bastille because

A. the citizens were attacking strongly.
B. his soldiers sided with the citizens.
C. his bluff failed.
D. of none of these reasons.

Directions: Complete this statement.

(SM) **3.** A good title for this passage would be

____

65

Why was the Bastille important to the citizens of Paris? The building of the Bastille had been started in 1370 under Charles V. By the seventeenth century it had ceased to be important for defense. Cardinal Richelieu turned it into a prison. It was not an ordinary prison to punish common crimes. Its huge doors closed only on enemies of the King. The Bastille's workings were secret. Prisoners were taken to it in closed carriages. Soldiers on guard duty had to stand with their faces to the wall. No talking was allowed. Worst of all, a prisoner never knew if he would be there a day, a week, a year, or forever. Only the King's letter could set him free.

Over the years the number of arrests by King's letter had become fewer. By the time of its fall, most of the prisoners were writers who had written against the corrupt deeds of the government. Voltaire, the famous French writer, spent a year there in 1717-1718, and another 12 days in 1726.

For those who believed in free speech and free thinking, the Bastille stood for everything evil. The day it was captured, the "Conquerors of the Bastille" found only seven prisoners inside. None the less, the Bastille was hated by the people. It was a symbol of the King's complete power.

PASSAGE 65 QUESTIONS

Directions: Circle **True** or **False.**

(D) **1.** Since the time of Charles V in the fourteenth century, the Bastille had been a prison. True False

(D) **2.** Anyone who did something wrong could find himself suddenly in the Bastille. True False

(G) **3.** As a prison, everything done in it was done in secret. True False

(G) **4.** The King could put people in, or let them go out, as he wanted. True False

(G) **5.** At the time it was captured, there were so few prisoners in it that it meant little to the people. True False

Directions: Which choice best completes the thought? Circle the letter.

(SM) **6.** This passage's main purpose is to

A. tell a story.

B. tell about interesting characters.
C. show the inner workings of the Bastille.
D. try to prove a point.

66

But why did the fall of the Bastille lead to the surrender of the Monarchy and the victory of the French Revolution? The fall of the Bastille was brought about because the soldiers guarding it refused to fight the people. Three weeks before two companies of the Garde Francaise had refused to go on duty. Four days later, other soldiers joined the citizens, saying they would never fight the people of Paris. And seventy-five members of the Swiss Guard went over to the Revolution just before the Bastille was stormed.

Thus, de Launay surrendered because his men inside refused to fight. He knew he would get no help from the army outside. So the Bastille fell because the army in Paris joined the citizens, and not because of the bravery of the attackers. Its fall showed the people that the army was with them. From the day it fell, the King and his nobles had no choice but to give up.

PASSAGE 66 QUESTIONS

Directions: Circle the letter of the choice that best completes each thought below.

(G) **1.** The Bastille fell because
A. of the bravery of the attackers.
B. the army would not help de Launay.
C. the nobles gave up.
D. the soldiers guarding it refused to fight.

(G) **2.** The monarchy fell because
A. the Bastille fell.
B. the fall of the Bastille showed that the army was with the people.
C. the people fought it.
D. de Launay surrendered.

(SM) **3.** This passage—part 3 of the Bastille story—is mainly meant to explain
A. why the Revolution was won.
B. how the army acted.
C. how the Bastille fell.
D. what the fall of the Bastille had to do with the people's victory.

VOCABULARY REMINDER CHECK-TESTS

Directions:
1. Each test begins with a list of words. Say each word aloud. If you pronounce the word correctly, circle the √. If you get it wrong, circle the X.
2. Some words are in bold print in sentences. Mark each sentence **True** or **False** by circling T or F.

TEST NO. 1

Passage Number							
2, 3	**a.** imaginary	√	X	**b.** arthritis	√	X
3	**c.** slurp	√	X	**d.** knuckle	√	X
4	**e.** shepherd	√	X	**f.** Hercules	√	X

1 **g.** A **"stable"** of horses means where the horses are kept. T F

2 **h.** **Imaginary** tales are stories that are made up in someone's head. T F

3 **i.** If you have the **"willies,"** you are very calm and cool. T F

j. **Arthritis** is very bad for the joints in your body. T F

Circle the number of correct answers:
1 2 3 4 5 6 7 8 9 10

TEST NO. 2

5	**a.** shrugged	√	X	**b.** bayonet	√	X
5, 6	**c.** gauge	√	X	**d.** spinal	√	X
6	**g.** pier	√	X	**f.** prey	√	X

5 **h.** The **gauge** of a rifle has to do with how long it is. T F

6 **i.** **Cartilage** is the same thing as bone. T F

j. A **Doberman** is a large, strong dog. T F

Circle the number of correct answers:
1 2 3 4 5 6 7 8 9 10

TEST NO. 3

7	**a.** oxygen	√	X	**b.** machine	√	X
8, 9	**c.** rodeo	√	X	**d.** peculiar	√	X
9, 10	**e.** situation	√	X	**f.** harshly	√	X
10	**g.** grain	√	X	**h.** conflict	√	X

7 **i.** The **gunwhale** of a boat is what steers it. T F

9 **j.** A **vet** is a doctor who helps animals. T F

10 **k.** A **sheaf** of grain is a bundle of grain. T F

Circle the number of correct answers:
1 2 3 4 5 6 7 8 9 10

TEST NO. 4

Passage Number					
11	**a.** pasture	√	X	**b.** caravan	√
12	**c.** meanwhile	√	X	**d.** aide	√
	e. betray	√	X	**f.** Hebrew	√
	g. accused	√	X		

11 **h.** **Balsam** is something to eat. T

i. **Resin** comes from a tree. T

12 **j.** A **tunic** is a short outer garment. T

Circle the number of correct answer
1 2 3 4 5 6 7 8 9 1

TEST NO. 5

13	**a.** prisoner	√	X	**b.** Pharaoh	√
14	**c.** interpret	√	X	**d.** reveal	√
	e. famine	√	X	**f.** reserve	√
	g. chariot	√	X		
15	**h.** hostage	√	X	**i.** climax	√

14 **j.** A **sleek** person is fat. T

Circle the number of correct answer
1 2 3 4 5 6 7 8 9

TEST NO. 6

16	**a.** paralyzed	√	X	**b.** scientist	√
17	**c.** astronaut	√	X	**d.** fluid	√
	e. gravity	√	X		
18	**f.** nephew	√	X	**g.** aunt	√

16 **h.** A **mammal** feeds its young with milk. T

i. You **tweak** noses. T

j. **Biologists** study buildings. T

Circle the number of correct answe
1 2 3 4 5 6 7 8 9

TEST NO. 7

18	**a.** relative	√	X	**b.** bugle	√
18,19	**c.** praise	√	X	**d.** medical	√
19	**e.** cyano-acrylic	√	X		
19,20	**f.** surgeon	√	X	**g.** mystery	√
20	**h.** social	√	X	**i.** confuse	√

j. A **vocal** person is quiet. T

Circle the number of correct answe
1 2 3 4 5 6 7 8 9

Passage Number

TEST NO. 8

,21 **a.** silence ✓ X **b.** tennis ✓ X

c. relax ✓ X **d.** growl ✓ X

e. wheelbarrow ✓ X

f. American ✓ X

g. American League ✓ X

h. The mouth is a **feature** of the face. T F

i. Mammals **suckle** their young. T F

j. A **species** is a class or group of animals with many features that are alike. T F

Circle the number of correct answers:
1 2 3 4 5 6 7 8 9 10

TEST NO. 9

a. valuable ✓ X **b.** language ✓ X

c. oriental ✓ X **d.** monument ✓ X

e. pyramids ✓ X **f.** Sanskrit ✓ X

g. pleasure ✓ X **h.** modest ✓ X

i. undertaker ✓ X

j. A **scholar** knows a lot. T F

Circle the number of correct answers:
1 2 3 4 5 6 7 8 9 10

TEST NO. 10

a. ostrich ✓ X **b.** delivery ✓ X

,24 **c.** shunt ✓ X **d.** Haitian ✓ X

e. Congo ✓ X **f.** zombie ✓ X

g. A **thoroughbred** horse comes from carefully picked parents. T F

h. A **stallion** is a male horse. T F

i. A **mare** is a female horse. T F

j. A **gelding** cannot mate. T F

Circle the number of correct answers:
1 2 3 4 5 6 7 8 9 10

TEST NO. 11

a. corpse ✓ X **b.** shunned ✓ X

c. lustily ✓ X **d.** classic ✓ X

e. ego ✓ X **f.** flinch ✓ X

g. image ✓ X

h. A **sorcerer** uses exact science. T F

i. A **trance** is like a sleep. T F

j. An actor's **heyday** is the time he is most popular. T F

Circle the number of correct answers:
1 2 3 4 5 6 7 8 9 10

Passage Number

TEST NO. 12

27,28 **a.** famous ✓ X **b.** deserve ✓ X

28 **c.** happen ✓ X **d.** paragraph ✓ X

e. recall ✓ X **f.** posture ✓ X

28,29 **g.** listening ✓ X **h.** Virginia ✓ X

i. Pennsylvania ✓ X

27 **j.** A person's **style** is the way he does things; his dress, habits, gestures, and talk all go to make up his style. T F

Circle the number of correct answers:
1 2 3 4 5 6 7 8 9 10

TEST NO. 13

29 **a.** Shenandoah ✓ X

b. treason ✓ X **c.** militia ✓ X

d. fizzle ✓ X **e.** colonel ✓ X

30 **f.** concentration ✓ X

g. tournament ✓ X

h. envelope ✓ X

i. computer ✓ X

j. positive ✓ X

Circle the number of correct answers:
1 2 3 4 5 6 7 8 9 10

TEST NO. 14

30,31 **a.** rarely ✓ X **b.** command ✓ X

c. thigh ✓ X **d.** athlete ✓ X

e. hooves ✓ X **f.** custom ✓ X

32 **g.** rattlesnake ✓ X **h.** advanced ✓ X

30 **i.** To be **aloof** is to be close to people. T F

31 **j.** A **bridle path** is a special path for hikers. T F

Circle the number of correct answers:
1 2 3 4 5 6 7 8 9 10

TEST NO. 15

32 **a.** development ✓ X

b. necessary ✓ X

c. photography ✓ X

d. retractable ✓ X

e. counterattack ✓ X

f. embed ✓ X

g. hypodermic ✓ X

33 **h.** Missouri ✓ X

32 **i.** **Venom** is good for digestion. T F

j. An **impact** is hardly felt. T F

Circle the number of correct answers:
1 2 3 4 5 6 7 8 9 10

Passage Number

TEST NO. 16

33,34 **a.** musket ✓ X **b.** reservation ✓ X
34,35 **c.** fuel ✓ X **d.** geologist ✓ X
36,37 **e.** basic ✓ X **f.** loyal ✓ X
37 **g.** hyena ✓ X **h.** alert ✓ X
34 **i.** **Conflict** means peace. T F
j. A **skirmish** is a short fight in a war. T F

Circle the number of correct answers:
1 2 3 4 5 6 7 8 9 10

TEST NO. 17

38 **a.** victory ✓ X **b.** mechanic ✓ X
39 **c.** molasses ✓ X
37 **d.** A **gagman** makes people cry. T F
e. A **cult** is an in-group. T F
f. A **ritual** can be part of a religion. T F
38 **g.** A **panzer** is a foot-soldier group in an army. T F
h. A **cipher** is a secret. T F
i. An **enigma** is a puzzle. T F
j. To **intercept** is to miss contact. T F

Circle the number of correct answers:
1 2 3 4 5 6 7 8 9 10

TEST NO. 18

39 **a.** molasses ✓ X **b.** medicine ✓ X
c. moist ✓ X **d.** licorice ✓ X
40 **e.** muscle-tone ✓ X
41 **f.** addict ✓ X **g.** legal ✓ X
39 **h.** A **lozenge** is a place to rest. T F
i. An **extract** is a part, not a whole. T F
40 **j.** To **preen** is to neglect one's looks. T F

Circle the number of correct answers:
1 2 3 4 5 6 7 8 9 10

TEST NO. 19

41 **a.** interest ✓ X **b.** methadone ✓ X
c. heroin ✓ X **d.** educational ✓ X
e. A **devoted** son helps his parents. T F
f. A **clinic** is a place where sick people go for help. T F
g. Some people have no **tolerance** for coffee; coffee bothers them. T F
h. Methadone prevents **highs** of heroin. T F
i. **Barbiturates** hop you up. T F
j. **Cocaine** is a candy. T F

Circle the number of correct answers:
1 2 3 4 5 6 7 8 9 10

Passage Number

TEST NO. 20

42 **a.** fussy ✓ X **b.** difference ✓
c. imitate ✓ X **d.** bartender ✓
e. social ✓ X **f.** favorite ✓
g. phonies ✓ X **h.** pillar ✓
43 **i.** primitive ✓ X
41 **j.** **Amphetamine** is a drug taken through the nose. T

Circle the number of correct answe
1 2 3 4 5 6 7 8 9

TEST NO. 21

43 **a.** courage ✓ X **b.** superstition ✓
c. normal ✓ X **d.** information ✓
e. prefer ✓ X **f.** untrained ✓
44 **g.** defensive ✓ X
h. fainthearted ✓ X
45,46 **i.** terror ✓ X **j.** oxygen ✓

Circle the number of correct answe
1 2 3 4 5 6 7 8 9

TEST NO. 22

47 **a.** failure ✓ X **b.** conditions ✓
48 **c.** customs ✓ X **d.** wrestling ✓
e. judge ✓ X **f.** cushion ✓
g. bouts ✓ X **h.** outlooks ✓
i. colored ✓ X
46 **m.** An **eerie** is an eagle's nest. T

Circle the number of correct answe
1 2 3 4 5 6 7 8 9

TEST NO. 23

48 **a.** orange ✓ X **b.** organizes ✓
49 **c.** badge ✓ X **d.** tradition ✓
50 **e.** rival ✓ X **f.** dodge ✓
g. concentrate ✓ X
51 **h.** thrust ✓ X **i.** grapple ✓
50 **j.** **Leverage** means extra power. T

Circle the number of correct answer
1 2 3 4 5 6 7 8 9

TEST NO. 24

51,52 **a.** victory ✓ X **b.** century ✓
c. wheat ✓ X **d.** protein ✓
53 **e.** prey ✓ X **f.** loneliness ✓
g. misadventure ✓ X
h. hot-tempered ✓ X
i. **Scribbling** is hard to read. T
j. A **privateer** is a privately-owned ship. T

Circle the number of correct answer
1 2 3 4 5 6 7 8 9 1

TEST NO. 25

Passage Number									
3	**a.**	quarrel	✓	X	**b.**	imagination	✓	X
	c.	politics	✓	X	**d.**	heroine	✓	X
3,54	**e.**	peopled	✓	X	**f.**	temple	✓	X
4	**g.**	priest	✓	X	**h.**	purple	✓	X
	i.	degree	✓	X	**j.**	businessman	✓	X

Circle the number of correct answers:
1 2 3 4 5 6 7 8 9 10

TEST NO. 26

4	**a.**	trench	✓	X	**b.**	confidence	✓	X
	c.	fierce	✓	X	**d.**	Japanese	✓	X
5	**e.**	marble	✓	X	**f.**	previous	✓	X
	g.	ambassador	✓	X				

4 **h.** A **rite** is part of a ritual. T F
i. A **Buddhist** follows the teachings of Mao-Tse-Tung. T F
j. To **chant** is to repeat in a singing voice. T F

Circle the number of correct answers:
1 2 3 4 5 6 7 8 9 10

TEST NO. 27

6	**a.**	famous	✓	X	**b.**	shilling	✓	X
	c.	misery	✓	X	**d.**	sergeant	✓	X
	e.	patient	✓	X	**f.**	logical	✓	X
7	**g.**	elephant	✓	X	**h.**	argument	✓	X
	i.	creature	✓	X				

6 **j.** **Psychological** problems have to do with a person's mind. T F

Circle the number of correct answers:
1 2 3 4 5 6 7 8 9 10

TEST NO. 28

7	**a.**	creature	✓	X	**b.**	experience	✓	X
7,58	**c.**	Israeli	✓	X	**d.**	experiment	✓	X
8	**e.**	scholar	✓	X	**f.**	shepherd	✓	X
	g.	scroll	✓	X	**h.**	Jerusalem	✓	X

i. **Parchment** was written on. T F
j. **Papyrus** was a plant from which ink was made. T F

Circle the number of correct answers:
1 2 3 4 5 6 7 8 9 10

TEST NO. 29

9	**a.**	Bible	✓	X	**b.**	Middle Ages	✓	X
	c.	contract	✓	X	**d.**	marriage	✓	X
	e.	divorce	✓	X	**f.**	property	✓	X
	g.	commander	✓	X				
0	**h.**	superior	✓	X	**i.**	geared	✓	X

9 **j.** A **zealot** is a quiet, calm person. T F

Circle the number of correct answers:
1 2 3 4 5 6 7 8 9 10

TEST NO. 30

Passage Number								
60	**a.**	timid	✓	X	**b.**	self-image	✓	X
	c.	label	✓	X	**d.**	assertive	✓	X
	e.	aggressive	✓	X				
61	**f.**	inhuman	✓	X	**g.**	neighbor	✓	X
	h.	emergency	✓	X				

60 **i.** If you have **self-esteem**, you have confidence. T F
j. To **assert** yourself means to give in. T F

Circle the number of correct answers:
1 2 3 4 5 6 7 8 9 10

TEST NO. 31

61	**a.**	middle-aged	✓	X
	b.	conditioned	✓	X
	c.	responsible	✓	X
	d.	researcher	✓	X
	e.	receptionist	✓	X
	f.	file cabinet	✓	X
	g.	emotional	✓	X
62	**h.**	secretary	✓	X
	i.	judgment	✓	X

61 **j.** **Diabetes** is good for you. T F

Circle the number of correct answers:
1 2 3 4 5 6 7 8 9 10

TEST NO. 32

63	**a.**	adjust	✓	X	**b.**	sensitive	✓	X
	c.	history	✓	X	**d.**	attitude	✓	X
	e.	sensation	✓	X	**f.**	unpleasant	✓	X
64	**g.**	government	✓	X				

62 **h.** A **layout** is a plan. T F
63 **i.** **Novocaine** makes nerves tender. T F
j. A **fakir** often begs. T F

Circle the number of correct answers:
1 2 3 4 5 6 7 8 9 10

TEST NO. 33

64	**a.**	pellet	✓	X
	b.	commander	✓	X
	c.	Bastille	✓	X
64,65	**d.**	conqueror	✓	X
	e.	corrupt	✓	X
	f.	ammunition	✓	X
	g.	seventeeth	✓	X
64	**h.**	monarchy	✓	X

i. A **garrison** is a place where soldiers stay. T F
j. A **symbol** stands for something. T F

Circle the number of correct answers:
1 2 3 4 5 6 7 8 9 10

A MODEL VOCABULARY NOTEBOOK PAGE

1. Keep a special notebook just for vocabulary building.
2. Find a new word each day.
3. In your notebook, write the sentence in which you found the word.
4. Underline the word.
5. Look up the word in the dictionary. Write the meaning that fits the way the word was used in your sentence.

Example: *So, if you want to go on popping your knuckles, Dr. Swezey says it's O.K.*

(Sentence in which the word was seen)

knuckle: a joint of a finger

(Meaning of the word as used in the sentence)

1. ____________________

____

(Sentence in which the word was seen)

____

(Meaning of the word as used in the sentence)

2. ____________________

____

(Sentence in which the word was seen)

____

(Meaning of the word as used in the sentence)

3. ____________________

____

(Sentence in which the word was seen)

____

(Meaning of the word as used in the sentence)

HOW TO CHART YOUR COMPREHENSION PROGRESS:

(Read this after you have done your first passage of the 66.)

Let's say that you did the questions on Passage 1, and you got 5 answers right.

If you look at the COMPREHENSION PROGRESS CHART on the next page, you will see, at the bottom of the chart, a number for each Passage — from 1 to 66.

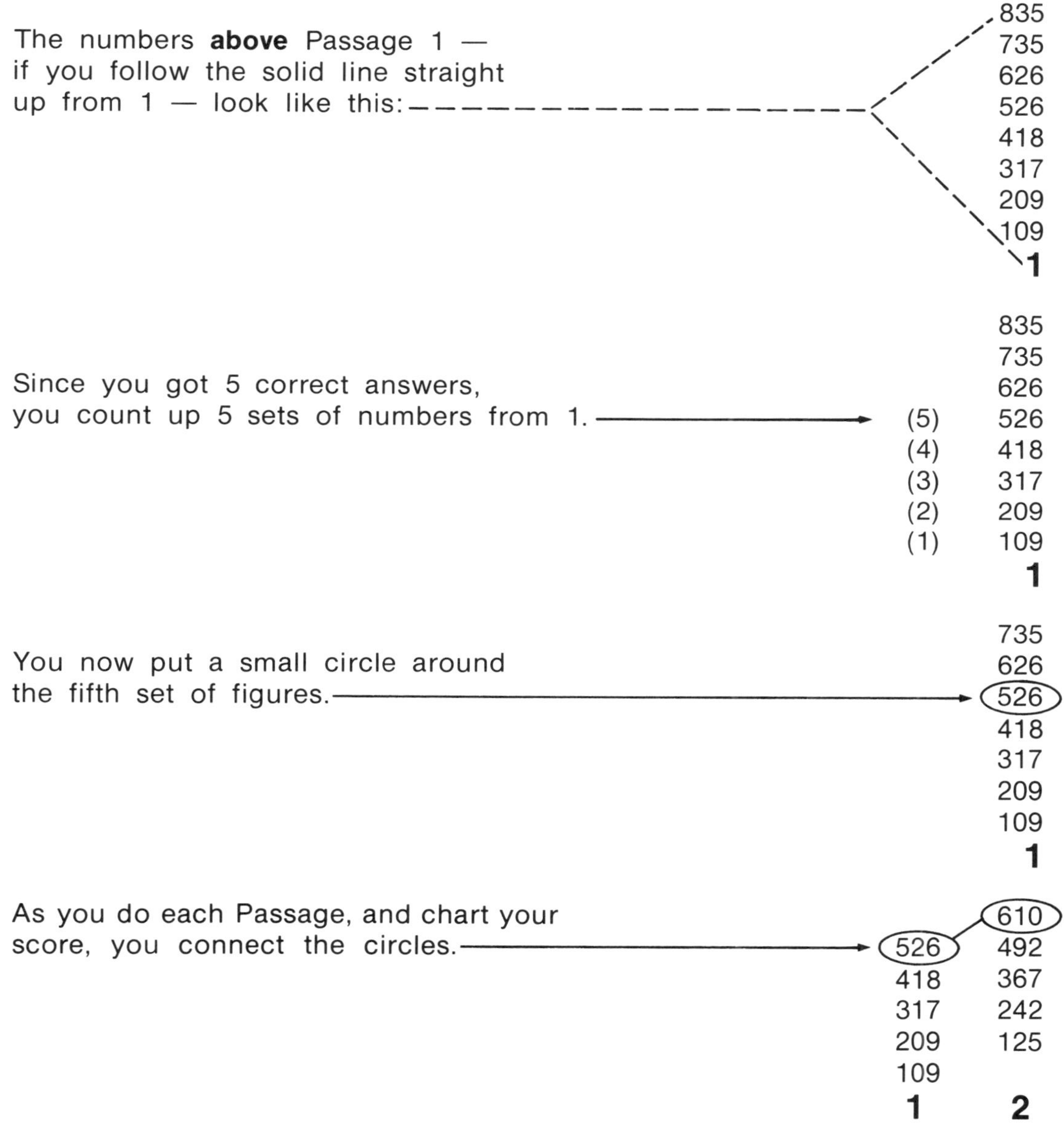

That's all there is to it.

The chart is built in a way to give you more credit for harder passages. So that if you got 60% on Passage 12, for example, which is easy, you would circle 440 on the chart, but if you got 60% on Passage 46, which is harder, your same 60% would give you 521.

Let's hope that when you get to Passage 66, you will bat 1000!

COMPREHENSION

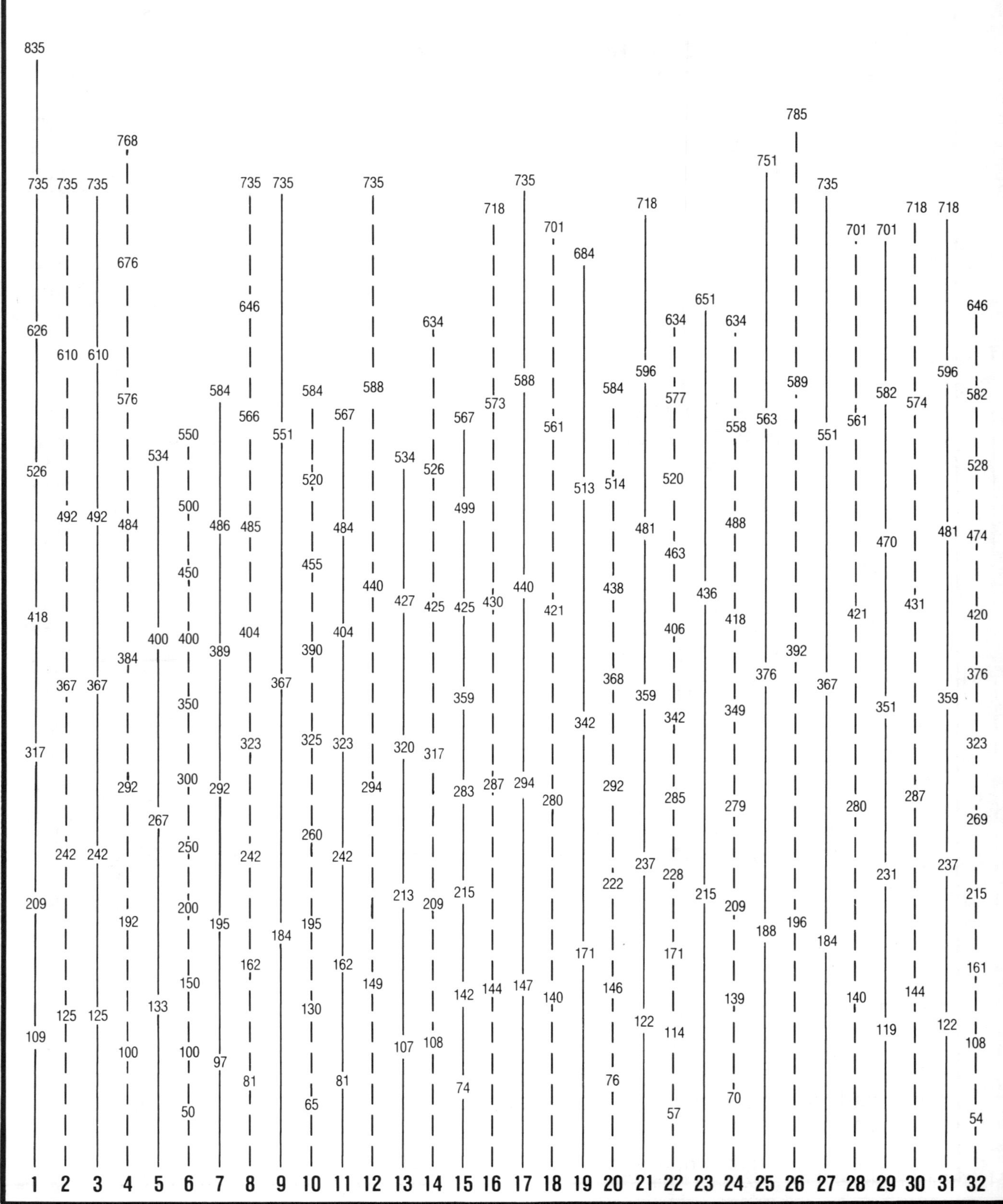

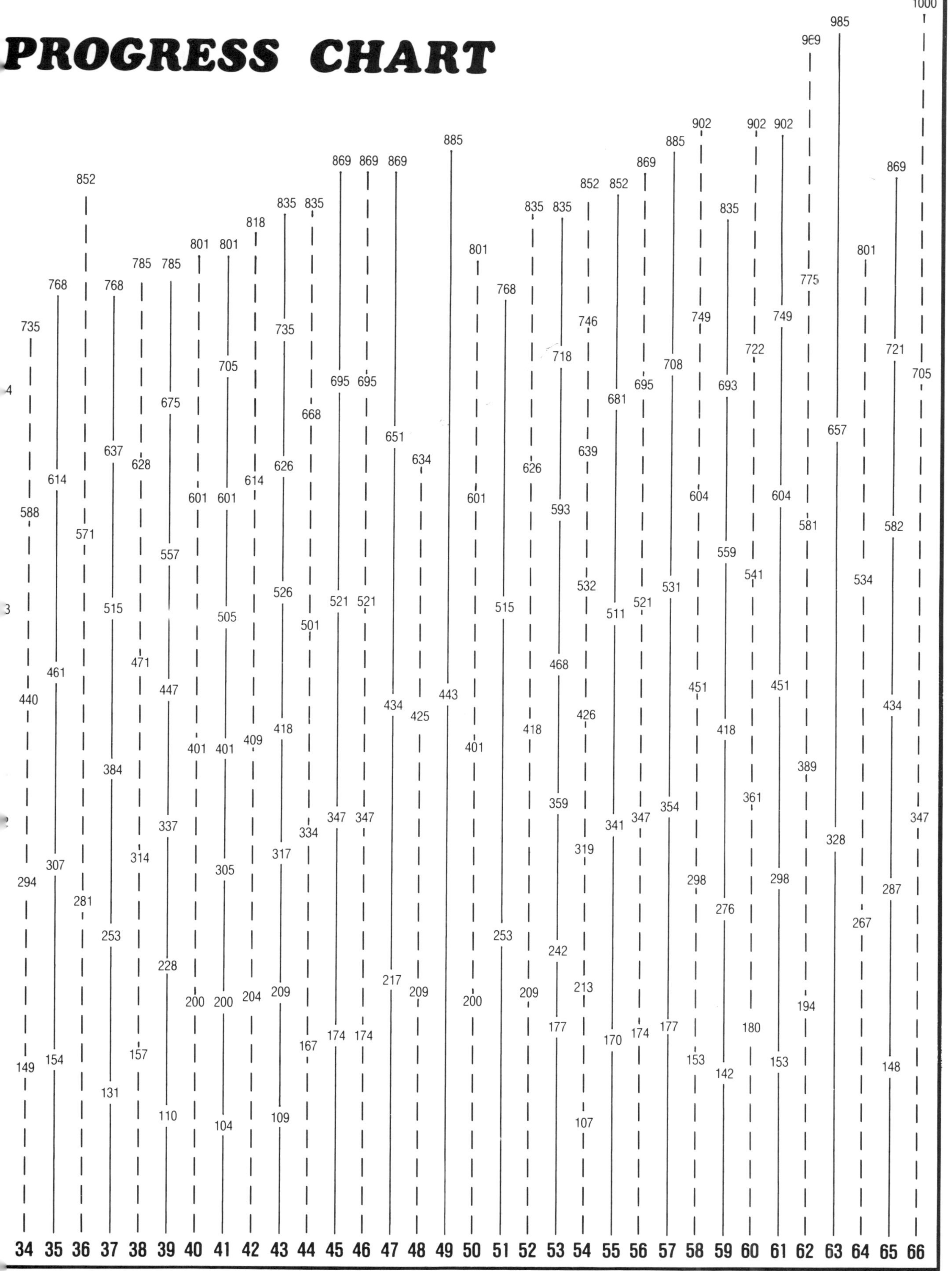
PROGRESS CHART
735 588 440 294 149
768 614 461 307 154
852 571 281
768 637 515 384 253 131
785 628 471 314 157
785 675 557 447 337 228 110
801 601 401 200
801 705 601 505 401 305 200 104
818 614 409 204
835 735 626 526 418 317 209 109
835 668 501 334 167
869 695 521 347 174
869 695 521 347 174
869 651 434 217
634 425 209
885 443
801 601 401 200
768 515 253
835 626 418 209
835 718 593 468 359 242 177
852 746 639 532 426 319 213 107
852 681 511 341 170
869 695 521 347 174
885 708 531 354 177
902 749 604 451 298 153
835 693 559 418 276 142
902 722 541 361 180
902 749 604 451 298 153
969 775 581 389 194
985 657 328
801 534 267
869 721 582 434 287 148
1000 705 347
34 35 36 37 38 39 40 41 42 43 44 45 46 47 48 49 50 51 52 53 54 55 56 57 58 59 60 61 62 63 64 65 66